# COMING *to* MY SENSES

# COMING *to* MY SENSES

### THE MAKING OF A COUNTERCULTURE COOK

## ALICE WATERS

*with*

Cristina Mueller & Bob Carrau

CLARKSON POTTER/PUBLISHERS
NEW YORK

ILLUSTRATION CREDITS
Alistair Laming/Alamy Stock Photo, p. 170; Eleanor Bertino, p. 81;
David Goines, pp. 129, 130, 137, 142, 143, 268; Elia Haworth, p. 229;
Chris Kjobech, The Oakland Tribune Collection, the Oakland Museum of
California, p. 88; Tom Luddy, p. 210; New York Daily News Archive/Getty
Images, p. 58; Nicolas Pagnol, CMF-MPC, pp. 261, 264; George Rinhart/
Corbis Historical/Getty Images, p. xii; Robert Scheer, p. 135; Gail Skoff,
p. 238; Charles and Lindsey Shere, pp. 154, 255, 280, 285; U.S.D.A. War
Food Administration, p. 30; Alice Waters, pp. 3, 4, 11, 18, 25, 27, 39, 46, 69,
96, 100, 102, 117, 120, 158, 159, 190, 194, 195, 204, 220, 224, 259, 294, 300.

Library of Congress Cataloging-in-Publication Data is available upon
request.

ISBN 978-0-307-71828-0
EBOOK ISBN 978-1-101-90665-1

Printed in the United States of America

Book design by Martha Blegen
Jacket design by Ian Dingman
Jacket photograph courtesy of David Goines

10  9  8  7  6  5  4  3  2  1

FIRST EDITION

*In memory of Mario Savio*

# CONTENTS

Here is how I cook: First I'm at the farmers' market, buying a bunch of French breakfast radishes, the purple-fringed lettuces, the spring garlic—I'm thinking about the state of the Blenheim apricots and the Santa Rosa plums. I'm looking for fruits and vegetables that are perfectly ripe, things that just came out of the ground or were just picked. I'm not necessarily thinking about how the ingredients will go together—I'm just responding to what I'm finding. It's a lot about aliveness, a lot about color, the smell of things, the look. . . . I'm listening to what the farmer has to say about what's going on in the fields. I think we forget sometimes that food is alive and that we have to follow that intuition and treat food as a living thing.

At this point, I don't quite know what I'm going to cook, and I'm not really putting the meal together. It's when I take the ingredients home, unpack them from my basket, and spread them out on the table in my kitchen—that's when I start imagining how the ingredients relate to one another and how they can come together to make a menu. I'm using all my senses. I'm smelling the garlic, tasting the pungency of the radishes and the tartness of the vinaigrette, feeling the firmness of the apricots; I'm thinking about the people who are going to sit at the table and what they like to eat, the courses following one another; what kind of day it is, whether it's cold outside and I want to light a fire in the fireplace, or whether it's warm and I want to sit outside by the herb garden. I'm improvising, trying to capture and express that moment in time. I'm letting my senses lead me. It's how we cook at Chez Panisse. It's how we've always cooked at Chez Panisse.

People want to know how I came to open a restaurant at twenty-seven years old. I never went to culinary school, I never cooked professionally. Why a restaurant? Why *this* kind of restaurant? Why this kind of cooking? How did I have the courage to open it? And the truth is, I'd never really thought about it deeply until now. I'm not a reflective person by nature. My answer has always been that I was disillusioned with politics and needed a way to make money, and I loved to cook and I thought I'd just open a little place for my friends, a refuge from the turbulent activity in the streets around us. And this is partly true but not the whole story. It doesn't completely explain how I came to be the young woman who opened Chez Panisse, how I learned to do what I did. When I think about my past, I see that the way I was raised and the experiences I had as a young woman fed and formed me in such profound ways that opening a

place like Chez Panisse was in a sense inevitable. My childhood and young adulthood, it turned out, held the seeds of
my own edible education, the values that empowered me to
gather a group of like-minded friends and open the doors—
barely!—of a little French restaurant in Berkeley, California,
in 1971. And though I didn't think about it much back then,
that little French restaurant on its opening night held not
only the important threads of my past but all the deep, idiosyncratic potential for what was to come.

# CHAPTER I

# Natural History

When I was little, I always wanted to go to the Museum of Natural History and eat at the Automat for my birthday. So my family took the train from Chatham, New Jersey, to the Hoboken ferry into New York City. It was only for special events that we'd do this; we didn't usually eat out at restaurants, and we didn't go to Manhattan much. But I loved New York City. The dioramas in the natural history museum were magical to me. I liked seeing the animals in their homes, liked that I could get up close to them: the hummingbirds nestled in their tiny nests, the lions with their cubs on the Serengeti Plain, the little zebra foals. These were all exotic worlds that I knew nothing about.

We'd get all dressed up for our outings. My sister Ellen and I usually wore something my father's sister Doris had made. Aunt Doris was an artist and often sewed clothes for us. My favorite was a cotton turquoise dress with a little pink flower print, pearly buttons at the neck, and a satin sash that tied in a bow at the back.

After the museum, we would take the subway to the Automat in Times Square. It was the first restaurant I remember going to; I must have been six or seven. Why was it my favorite? Because I could choose my own food. I can picture myself standing there in the middle of the restaurant, my pockets filled with quarters. Every surface of the Automat was shiny: there was a huge wall of little stainless steel doors, sort of like post office boxes, with windows displaying the food in each one. You put your money in one of the post office box slots, opened the door, and got your dish. Through the little door, you could catch a glimpse of someone cutting lemon meringue pie or assembling tuna salad sandwiches in the kitchen behind. It felt like an entirely new way to have food. I'd range around in front of the stainless steel wall and choose my dishes. Nothing was wrapped in paper, and I liked seeing the food before I picked what I wanted—I couldn't or didn't read the menu, so being able to see it resonated with me. We'd each go for what we wanted, and then the whole family met back at the table to eat our various dishes together. I loved being given my own money and the fact that I could choose exactly what I wanted. At home we always had to eat what was put in front of us, but I loved putting my money into that little door—it was my own choice. (The great irony is that Chez Panisse became known for offering just one fixed-price menu each night—no choice at all. But more on that later.)

.   .   .

My parents had moved to our home on Passaic Avenue in Chatham just before I was born. The house was quite old, a little wooden clapboard structure from the late 1800s with a pitched roof and slanted ceilings in the two bedrooms upstairs. The family didn't have a car until I was four, and the story I was told every year on my birthday was that when my mother went into labor with me, my father was so worried she wouldn't get to the hospital in time that he put her on the milk train—a local freight train that carried the milk from the dairy farms to the milkmen in town. My mother

boarded the train all by herself; my father needed to borrow a car, pack up an overnight bag from home, and arrange for someone to watch my older sister Ellen, so my mother rode the milk train alone, in heavy labor. It was all men around her, and she was seriously worried that I was going to be born on the train that delivered the milk. Thank God she made it to the hospital—just barely.

The Passaic Avenue house was what you might call a fixer-upper. It was in constant need of repairs, with holey screen doors that let the mosquitoes in and peeling wallpaper. My father was forever painting and putting the paper back up on the walls—I can still smell the wallpaper paste. It was drafty in winter, and I was always cold. On winter mornings my parents had to stoke the furnace in the basement; it was the only place in the whole house that was warm enough, and I'd get dressed down there in front of the furnace while my father or mother shoveled coal. My fascination with fires might have first started there, but I think fire is fascinating to all kids.

When I was four, just a month after my sister Laura was born, Ellen and I came down with scarlet fever at the same time; we were quarantined to keep us from infecting the new baby. My mother was so worried about all of us. This was right before the polio vaccine was discovered, and people were paranoid about childhood diseases—no one fully understood where they came from or how to control them, and so many children died of scarlet fever in the first half of the twentieth century. It must have been particularly frightening for my mother, because her own mother had died of influenza when she was young. Baby Laura was sequestered downstairs in the dining room, which was turned into a makeshift nursery (my parents painted it Pepto-Bismol pink), and Ellen and I were kept upstairs in the slant-roofed bedroom we shared. There was a QUARANTINE sign posted on our front door, and my mother wore a mask around us. Fortunately, Baby Laura never caught it. Ellen and I kept getting in trouble because we were supposed to be in bed and not jumping around. But I did feel very sick, too. I don't remember much else from our time at that house, other than the big garden out back. When I was about five, we moved to another house in Chatham, on Van Doren Avenue, which was much more of a traditional 1950s house: new and white, with green shutters and a garage.

. . .

When I think about my sisters, the first thing that comes to mind is that I didn't know them very well. There were four years between my older sister Ellen and me, and between my younger sister Laura and me—and then my youngest sister Susan was two years younger than Laura. Laura and Susan were together in one bedroom, and Ellen and I shared the other. Ellen thought I was a mess—she never wanted to share a room with me and would get so upset about me throwing my clothes on the floor. I maintained a big rock collection for years; geodes were my obsession. It fascinated me that you could break a rock apart and discover it was filled with crystals, and I loved knowing about the layers of sandstone and quartz, being able to recognize them out on walks. I had shoeboxes full of rocks I'd bought or collected along the river.

Ellen wasn't thrilled about having all those rocks in our room, either. She was bossy, always—she had the upper hand, and she used it. We were so different in personality; I was emotional, my side of the bedroom was such a mess, and she was so practical, such a good student. I didn't like her much when we were young, mostly because she didn't want to be with me. We got into some vicious girl fights, biting and hair pulling. But in the way of so many younger siblings, I looked up to her. I always thought I'd end up like her: practical, a good student, responsible.

When you're young, four years is a huge difference in age. Ellen was much more grown up than I was, and Laura and Susan were babies, so my sisters and I didn't play to-gether much. I often felt sort of lonely at home. Susan and Laura had each other to play with, they were only two years apart, and Ellen was with her older friends and was closer to my parents. She seemed to have more to talk about with them, being the oldest child. She always got to sit in the front seat of our green Plymouth, while I had to sit in the backseat with the two babies.

Susan and Ellen were redheads, and Laura and I had brown hair. (My Irish grandmother, my father's mother, had the red hair in the family.) When I was little and Susan and Laura were still babies, I definitely thought I looked like my dad and Ellen looked more like my mother. I thought Ellen and my mother were sort of aligned, and my dad and I were more alike. (It's hard to say if that was real, though, since those were just ideas that came to my mind as a six- or seven-year-old. What was the truth, really?) I do know my dad always called me Princess, which may have annoyed the rest of my sisters. Maybe it was because I behaved like one. I was outspoken and had strong opinions—and they were irritating opinions: "I'm *not* eating this! I'm *not* doing that! I want shoes that look like *that*!" I was demanding, and if I didn't get what I wanted . . . well, you know. I had more of a temper than the other girls.

Sometimes I was sent to my room and put in my closet until I could behave; occasionally my father would give me a whack or two on the bottom with the back of his hand, but nothing very meaningful. And my mother never spanked me. I'd be punished for not cleaning my room, not washing the dishes, being mean to my sisters, all of the above, but mostly I was punished for arguing back. We four girls were always bickering at the dinner table—I thought we'd drive my father crazy. When he wanted peace and quiet, someone was always whining, "I don't want to go do my homework!" "I don't want to be sitting next to Laura, I want to be by Mom." "No, *I* want to be by Mom." "I like *that* chair!" "No, *I* sat in it first. *No!*" Really important stuff.

I spent a lot of time alone in my closet—both enforced and by choice. I was fascinated with *Captain Video and His Video Rangers*: you could mail in for a little rocket from Captain Video, and if you put the rocket under a lamp, it would glow in the dark. I'd go into the closet, turn off the lights, and set it off in there so I could see the rocket glowing. There was a small launcher for it, and the rocket would shoot up high, glowing yellow all the way up to the closet ceiling, or into the depths of the snowsuits stored on the shelves above. I mailed in for a space helmet from Captain Video, too, and I'd climb trees in it. I loved climbing trees—I still do!—and almost killed myself jumping out of the high branches of the willows in my backyard, wearing that helmet. (I have a beautiful giant redwood tree in my backyard right now. I keep thinking I'll create a little high platform in it where I can climb a rope ladder and sit, so I can be up there in the life of my tree.)

I think my father really wanted a son, so I slid into that role in the family. I liked to play with boys and played baseball every day after school with boys from the neighborhood. My childhood hero was Mickey Mantle. I loved him, and loved singing "I Love Mickey," Teresa Brewer's hit song about him. I always wanted to be the pitcher, even though I wasn't the best at it. The boys gave in to me eventually—I was unrelenting and wouldn't get off the mound—and after a while it was my designated position. I liked being pitcher because you're in the game all the time and at the center of things. We played every day after school, in the playground of Milton Avenue Grammar School—I wouldn't see my sisters until dinnertime.

For all my grammar school years, I played with the boy next door, Robert. There was a high sand pile between our houses, and we used to play on it with little cars: driving up the mountain, parking the cars, careening back down the mountain again. It was so easy to sit there barefoot in the sand with Robert, so comfortable. It was complete fantasy play, making a whole little town: "That's my house, this house is yours, I'll drive over and see you at your house." I remember that absolutely vividly, playing in the sand.

I wasn't into dolls. I had a stuffed rabbit named Rabbi that I slept with growing up, but not a lot more than that—I was much more of a tomboy. What I really thought I was was a cowboy—there's a picture of my sisters and me from one

Christmas in the 1950s, where everyone else is in dresses under the Christmas tree playing with their new dolls, and I'm standing there grinning in the head-to-toe cowboy outfit I'd been given. When I had my tonsils out at six years old, before we had a television set, my mother brought the record player into my room, and I listened to Roy Rogers's "Lonesome Cowboy Blues" over and over and cried, eating my ice cream. I loved sad cowboy songs. There was a loneliness and a freedom about them that I responded to: getting away on your horse, out there in the wilderness. After my parents got a television, I watched some early cowboy movies, with Hopalong Cassidy, Gene Autry, and Roy Rogers. (A small part of me wished for a cowboy to come take me away. In the 1950s, we were all very much in the place of "someday my prince will come"—that idea that someone would ride up on a horse, take you away, and love you.)

Those cowboy songs weren't limited to the record players, and I wasn't the only one who liked them. When we all piled in the car for a long drive, like when we were going to see my mother's family in Atlantic City, we sang cowboy songs—my father, my mother, my sisters, and I would all sing. My mother had been a singer when she was younger and so had a good voice and kept us on the melody and in tune. And my father, while not the most gifted vocalist, was always very enthusiastic—he totally got into it. Those were some of the happiest times I had with my family. We sang "Home on the Range," and the kids learned all the songs

from my parents' alma maters, Rutgers and New Jersey College for Women: "On the banks of the old Raritan, my boys, where old Rutgers evermore shall stand!" And we sang other old-fashioned songs, too: "She'll be coming round the mountain when she comes!" And "Way down upon the Swanee River, far, far away—there's where my heart is turning ever, there's where the old folks stay."

My parents were into big-band music and jazz—Benny Goodman, Duke Ellington, Glenn Miller, that whole period. I didn't like it. I preferred the sad cowboys, and I loved classical music—which is to say, I liked Tchaikovsky's *Nutcracker Suite*, the lone classical record my parents had along with all their big-band LPs. My sisters and I would listen to it all the time, all four girls dancing and putting on performances for my parents at their cocktail parties. But my parents adored jazz first and foremost, and the two of them would dance around our house to those records. My mother always loved dancing, and on special occasions my father would take her out to a nightclub to dance. Even years later, when they were much older and living in Berkeley, they'd go dancing at the Claremont Hotel when live bands were playing.

I loved music but didn't have a particular talent for creating it myself. My mother played the piano well, and Susan, too. We had a low Steinway spinet up against a wall in our house, and my father was obsessed with polishing that piano, even when it didn't need it, although he himself didn't play. I learned to play the piano when I was little but never practiced, and I can't play a thing now except "Für Elise" and "Chopsticks." I took violin lessons at school—or at least I did until they threw me out of the orchestra because I couldn't do the vibrato. But the idea of holding an instrument was something I really liked. When you got to carry an instrument home from school, it was like a sacred responsibility. I loved tucking my violin into its velvet box. It felt like something precious and valuable. (I feel the same way now about putting my knives into my knife case.) After that I took flute lessons in school until I was told I didn't have a talent for playing the flute because I didn't have enough breath.

I liked to hide out—*that* was my big talent. I liked to make little houses: taking the dining room chairs, draping blankets over them, and hiding underneath. And I was *really* good at hide-and-seek—seriously good. Because I've always understood volume surprisingly well, I have an innate sense of what will or will not fit into certain spaces. I always know whether this particular carton of milk will pour precisely into that particular bowl, just up to the rim without overflowing. I can get it spot on. And so I knew when my body could hide behind a couch and not be seen, or when it could fit inside a little cupboard—I knew exactly whether it would work. How useful is that?

I never ate lunch at the school cafeteria. I didn't want to: the food smelled bad, and it all looked brown. I don't remember anything there that was even identifiable as food. My mother would make me a paper bag lunch, or I would go home for lunch, since our house wasn't far away. I was very skinny and didn't like to eat much. The sandwiches my mother made me, things like peanut butter and bananas on whole wheat bread, were always dry, so sometimes I traded mine for my friends' cheese and bologna sandwiches on white bread. And grapes. I always had a bunch of grapes in there. My favorite lunch was a grilled cheese sandwich with pickles on the side. My mother made that from time to time when she was feeling indulgent, and when I was a little older, I'd have a grilled cheese sandwich and an orange soda at a dinette down the street when she wasn't watching.

*I've always loved cheese. I love it. I love that it has so many possibil-*
*ities, culinarily—from the little cheese in a taco to the whole myr-*
*iad of goat cheeses and French cheeses. And I think of grilled cheese*
*sandwiches as one of the great comfort foods. These days I make*
*them with a Cantal, a mountain cheese from France that's a little*
*like a Swiss—I like my cheese to be a bit tangy. I usually choose some*
*good whole wheat or levain bread from Acme Bread Company. I*
*slice the cheese and put it inside the bread, put some olive oil in a*
*cast iron pan—not too much!—drizzle oil on the top of the sand-*
*wich, and then weight it down with another cast iron pan. When it*
*gets really brown, I turn it over, and when the cheese starts to bubble*
*out the sides, I take it out. Then I rub both sides with half a clove of*
*garlic and serve it with a dill pickle or some sauerkraut (good home-*
*made sauerkraut, not the kraut out of the can that I never liked as a*
*child!). Or I'll have a little undressed salad on the side—the melted*
*cheese and the olive oil from the sandwich almost dress the lettuce.*
*Sometimes in the summer I'll put some hot peppers in the sandwich*
*or serve it with a tomato salad.*

I liked school, but I was not a particularly driven student in
any given subject—my grades were good, generally, but I
was distractible. I will say I don't remember studying very
hard. I had one extraordinary teacher in third grade, Mrs.
Mead, who really set the bar high. I just loved her; she'd
make up magical arts and crafts projects to go along with
whatever subject we were studying. Mrs. Mead was fascinated by birds and carved and painted them. She fashioned

a ruby-crowned kinglet and gave it to me—I still have that bird upstairs in my attic. She'd even take kids from the class out on the weekends, and we'd go on bird walks. I still know all the bird names from that time: goldfinch, cardinal, red-wing blackbird, towhee, sparrow, robin, oriole. She was an amazing, amazing teacher—I was so lucky. In fact, she just wrote to me—she's in her nineties now, and one of her kids came to Chez Panisse.

I talked to my friends too much, and the teachers would put me in the coatroom to punish me. The coat closet had these little vents, and I probably spent my whole fourth-grade year in there with the snowsuits, peering through the vents. Too bad I didn't have my rocket launcher with me.

I didn't like being alone. I liked being in my little hide-outs, being in my own world, but still feeling the presence of sisters or adults out there in the house around me. But I didn't like feeling that there was no one there to understand me. I remember standing alone once in the living room and looking out the window at Van Doren, at maybe ten or so, feeling *really* by myself—it was an existential moment. I was looking out the window feeling solitary and unhappy, with nobody to talk to, nobody to turn to. I can still see that window, with the filmy cream-colored rayon curtains and the hard winter landscape outside.

*I still don't like to be alone. When I see all these things around me in the world that are beautiful, I just want to* talk *to somebody about them—I want someone else to share in them, see them, smell them, taste them. I don't want to keep them to myself. It's not that I can't eat a meal by myself. I can. But I really like to sit down to a meal with a friend. There's something about having that enjoyment reflected back to you, when you can feel that mutualism, that shared understanding. I need that in my life. I do like companionable solitude, when other people are around but everyone is engaged in his or her own activity. And I can be alone—my favorite thing is puttering around the house by myself for three or four hours, following my inclination to take a book off the shelf, remember a recipe from it, put it back. It relaxes me. But I like knowing that I'm meeting someone for dinner at the end of it.*

I always had lots of friends and was very jealous when someone had more friends than I did. I had a bunch of innocent grade-school boyfriends—Bill Berghaus, Richard Ostram, Jack Guerrero. I liked different things about each of them, and I wanted all of them to pay attention to me. Sometimes they'd walk me to school or walk me home. They'd give me friendship rings, and I had to keep switching the rings according to which boyfriend I was talking to. I wanted all of them to like me the best, but I also wanted each of them to feel he had my undivided attention. Some things never change.

One year, maybe in fourth grade, the teacher asked all the students to say what they'd like to be when they grew up.

"I want to be a stewardess," I said.

"If you want to be a stewardess, you'll have to stand up

very straight and grow tall," my teacher said. It was a functional thing, she explained—I was the shortest one in the class, and a stewardess had to be tall enough to open the baggage compartments. (Needless to say, I'm still not tall enough to do that—I only made it to five foot two.) The teacher measured me against the wall to show me how much progress I needed to make toward my stewardess goal. But the truth was, I didn't feel terribly invested in this aspiration. I saw stewardesses in advertisements in *Life* magazine, and I thought they were a glamorous lot, with their smart dresses and their world traveling, and when my teacher asked, it had seemed as good an answer as any.

## MARGARET HICKMAN

*10 South Marion Avenue, Ventnor*

### POLITICAL SCIENCE

Petite and pretty, Mlle. Midge Hickman's fieriness in discussions of economics and politics is something to be wondered at, and shunned, moreover, by the slow-witted. Besides her ability in social sciences, she is also talented in music. A member of Music Guild, Choir, and Delta Mu, she carols through corridors of the French House and sings harmoniously at soirées. With equal gaiety and vim she designs new coiffures, tears about on her bike, and engages in a round of parties. We wonder whether she can be "toned down" even by domesticity—and hope not.

# CHAPTER 2

# Mother and Dad

This was the description of my mother Marge in her college yearbook. But it wasn't what I saw.

I have hands just like my mother's: small, but with long fingers. She had a gold ring she always wore with a black onyx stone in it, her class ring from New Jersey College for Women in Brunswick. I loved that NJC ring. It had a fir tree etched into it, and I thought it was very beautiful. My mother was naturally pretty, though she never spent money to dress herself up—that money was all for the kids. She wasn't stylish, but she looked good in clothes: she wore patterned housedresses that buttoned up the front and comfortable oxford shoes with socks—always comfortable shoes. She kept her wavy brown hair pulled back with bobby pins. I remember being on her lap, being held a lot—she was always that way with all of us kids, holding on to us.

She was very warm, very sweet, never scolding, just forever on our side. And yet she had strong opinions: "You *will* take those vitamins." "No, you *cannot* have an ice-cream cone." She could put her foot down and argue with my father about one thing or another, like what the family could afford to buy out of the Sears, Roebuck catalog. My mother didn't have a "real" job while we were growing up; she was gardening and canning and watching four girls and keeping the house together while my father was at work during the day. She was pretty overwhelmed most of the time—some days she could barely get food on the table and keep up with the wash, and she spent a lot of time at the ironing board. She was undoubtedly lonely. At night after dinner, she'd lie down with her feet up while we roughhoused with our father—she was tired a lot.

My mother was born in 1916, during World War I, in Atlantic City. Her mother, Edna Martha Wright, died of the Spanish flu when my mother was two. Edna's death broke my grandfather Frederick Hickman's heart. He was fighting in the war in France when she died, so my mother was sent to live with her maternal grandmother, and her newborn brother, Fred, was sent to live with my great-aunt Ina for a time. Two years later Frederick remarried a schoolteacher, Catherine, who he thought would be a good mother to his young children. As it turned out, Grandma Hickman—that's what we called her—was a very strict Baptist who wouldn't let my mother dance or read books at night or go to parties. When I say Baptist, I'm not talking about mainstream Southern Baptists; the fundamentalist Baptist Church *she* belonged to forbade smoking, drinking, dancing, and, from what I could see, smiling, too. My mother loved her father very much, but she never forgave him for his marriage to Grandma Hickman; it was hard for her to navigate that relationship. (To the end of her life, my mother could not forgive her father for refusing to dance with her at her wedding.)

My mother threw herself into her studies in school, and she was a Latin scholar and a very good pianist. She finally escaped her rigid home life to enroll at New Jersey College, where she majored in political science, took up smoking, and attended Communist Party meetings—she was a radical and often talked of changing the world. I think she got her lifelong political leftism from her father—he was a councilman in Atlantic City and liberal, surprising given the religious conservatism Grandma Hickman enforced at home. Despite whatever unhappiness my mother had about her father's union with Grandma Hickman, she looked up to him.

Somewhere along the way, at a fraternity dance for Lambda Chi at neighboring Rutgers University, Marge was set up with a Rutgers sophomore who was introduced to her as "Patty." She didn't like that name and told him she was going to call him Pat instead. In 1939 she married Pat Waters; she was twenty-three.

Pat and Marge Waters lived on a shoestring in New York City for a short time; they were in a fifth-floor walk-up on Maiden Lane in Greenwich Village, and my mother worked as a secretary or a low-level clerk, making seventeen dollars every two weeks. She knew next to nothing about cooking, by my father's account—"She didn't know how to boil water," he said. In 1940 she had her first baby, Ellen, and they moved to the New Jersey suburbs. In 1941 Frederick Hickman died of a heart attack. My mother was twenty-five.

Grandma Hickman outlived Frederick Hickman by quite a bit, and my family would visit her in Atlantic City during the summers. Grandma Hickman was a bit of a battle-ax—she wore only black and cooked only white food. I remember her wearing those black dresses and dark glasses; she was big, maybe a little dumpy, and not really affectionate with us. We had to behave, no question. For Christmas, she gave me bra strap extenders and discounted toothbrushes. But my mother felt a sense of obligation to her.

I don't know what it must have been like for my mother, at twenty-five, to be essentially an orphan—Grandma Hickman notwithstanding—but I do know that her marriage to my father was a solace to her. They had a very close relationship, and that was beautiful. Their affection for each other was evident. My father's response to so many situations was simply "Whatever Mother wants." He wanted her to feel supported, and the two of them were strong together, a united force. They were physically affectionate in their own way—not kissing on the lips (because nobody did that) but putting an arm around a shoulder or holding hands. They seemed, at least to all of us kids, to agree on most things. Or, you know, they'd argue about little stuff: my father would want to take us out for ice cream, and she'd say, "Oh, no you can't!" until eventually she'd relent and we'd go.

This was what my mother liked: She liked sitting out in the sun in the garden—she loved the flowers and vegetables we grew, and she enjoyed gardening, unlike me. (I only liked to pick.) She liked to go swimming, but not unless the water was warm—in that way, she was very much like me. She had a phobia of sailing (a pity, since my father was a good sailor) but liked the water and the beach. She liked to go for Sunday drives with my great-aunt Ina. She liked learning about health food—her passion for it was very big and made an impression on all of us. And she liked staying in bed—that would have been her dream, to do nothing in the morning. She used to tell us, "I just want to sleep in!" But, of course, she always had something to do, someone to take care of. Imagine you had to get up every day of your life and make breakfast and lunch for four kids—wouldn't you dream of having one day to sleep in?

My mother told me later that she had a nervous breakdown after having her last child—what we would call postpartum depression now. I think it was just too many kids, and she wasn't ready at that point to have another, especially since her next youngest was only two. "I was not a good mother at that time," she told me. She worried about how that affected us. I was six when it happened, in first grade, and the truth is, I don't have any memories of what it meant for us or if it affected me—I was in my solitary world around then, making forts and hiding in closets. As it happened, that bad case of tonsilitis I had was that first winter after Susan was born. I spent many days at home from school, and my mother remembers lying on the couch listening to that mournful cowboy record I loved so much and trying to deal with a crying baby, a two-year-old, and a sick six-year-old. She said later she should have sought professional help—but that was frowned upon at the time.

Instead, my mother's friend from college, Hope, came to help her out for a time while she was depressed. Hope was my mother's best friend. She named Ellen after her: Ellen Hope. Hope was very worldly and had lived in France and I got the benefit of that when I was little—my mother sang "Frère Jacques" to me, taught me to count to ten in French, and wished us *bonne nuit* or *bons rêves* when she kissed us good night. And when Hope moved to Tokyo, Ellen and I got kimonos and getas, the traditional red-lacquered wooden platform shoes, and we learned about Japan. When Hope wasn't abroad, she lived in Washington, D.C., where I think her husband was important in diplomatic circles; my mother and Hope saw each other as often as they could, but my mother was always wishing she lived nearer to us.

My mother was an avowed Democrat, and the poor and the downtrodden were constantly on her mind. When we didn't eat the food on our plates, she would remind us, "Remember the children who don't have enough to eat in India." She was the same way about clothes; she'd mend holes in our dresses instead of buying us new ones, or darn our socks. She had a lot of messages about conservation and about helping feed people—the idea that we should think of the people in the world who didn't have enough food to eat was very, very strong in our family.

I always thought of my mother as a radical, I did. Because of her, I had an Adlai Stevenson button pinned to my jacket, and I wore it to grammar school when *everybody* else was for Eisenhower—the other kids would go around singing, "Whistle while you work, Stevenson's a jerk, Eisenhower has more power, whistle while you work!" My mother was passionate about Stevenson. He was the Democratic nominee for president in 1952 and 1956, an intellectual humanist liberal, speaking out against McCarthyism and standing up for civil rights. He was a voice of reason, she said. And I was definitely conscious that my mother was the only person in the whole city of Chatham who was for him. She believed there was a limit to how much money

people should make, and above that they should be taxed 100 percent. How much more leftist can you be? My father was a conservative, and the two of them would often argue—and all the girls took my mother's side. So we were five women against my poor father.

*I remember right before my mother died at ninety-one, after my father had died and when her memory was beginning to go, she was sitting out in the yard with a big-brimmed lavender hat on. The sun was going down. I ducked in under her hat to kiss her, and she said, "I'm so proud of what you've done. All my life. You've lived the life I wanted to live." It was the last thing she said to me—she had a heart attack the next day. My mother.*

My father's name was Charles Allen Waters, but everybody called him Patty—a childhood nickname from when he was an Eagle Scout and would always be the last kid in line, hurrying to keep up: *pitter-pat, pitter-pat.* They'd all call out, "Here comes Patty!" He was born in Trenton, New Jersey, in 1915, the fifth of seven children. He sometimes felt he'd been born into the wrong family—he had darker skin and was more scholarly than the other children, and he was the first of his family to go to college.

Pat Waters was a tremendously hard worker. He was a human resources psychologist for the Prudential, a job he'd got right after college thanks to his older sister's husband;

he worked constantly and never took vacations until we were all older. Where my mother was very even-tempered and good-natured, my father was more introspective and a little unapproachable—not meaning to be that way, but just because he was so tired all the time. He was always immaculately dressed with an ironed handkerchief in his suit pocket and garters to hold up his socks. He would arrive at the Lackawanna train station in the evening, from Newark, and we'd pick him up. While we waited at the station for his train to arrive, I'd play under the mulberry trees near the tracks, hiding and playing house under the weeping branches. He would invariably be tired; once we got home, he'd pour himself a scotch and water, then another, and then he could tolerate us. Meanwhile my mother would be doing a million things, trying to get food on the table for dinner.

My father wasn't an intellectual. Neither of them was. They read the newspaper but didn't have a lot of books around. Later on when I started the restaurant, that was, I think, a big thing for me to work through: I was embarrassed by my father's lack of intellectualism. I thought his whole approach was just too naïve. But he was probably like me, working on his instincts—and by the end of his career, he was well respected in his field.

*My father briefly worked with us at the restaurant—he must have been about sixty-five at the time—after we opened the café in 1980. We'd been a group of thirty-five people till then, and now all of a sudden our number doubled. I was falling apart. He said, "Well, I'll come in and help you organize it." He was a business psychologist, after all—he knew how to do that—so I said, "Okay, Dad."*

*He came in and sat down with groups of us, worked with the dishwashers late at night, and learned all kinds of things about the restaurant. I was a bit embarrassed by his process. The last thing I wanted was a touchy-feely T-group of people working through their feelings. I don't even like talking about it—it was excruciating. His approach wasn't intellectual, and I had that hyperawareness of his flaws that every child has about his or her parents. I didn't want my colleagues to think badly of me because of my father, and I never liked sitting down and holding hands and talking through emotions, that kind of hippie mentality.*

*Of course, that was only my fear of what it would be—he wasn't* actually *asking them all to hold hands, though he did have these little role-playing activities. Even so, something about asking people to be emotionally intimate when they didn't want to be made me deeply uncomfortable—it seemed so contrived. It wasn't my way. And maybe some of it had to do with the emotional disconnect of the 1950s that I'd grown up with, that I didn't have the right vocabulary to talk about interpersonal relations—I'd rather do something to get to know someone. I'd rather be cooking and talking with them than being in therapy.*

*But the thing was, his methods made a big impression on people. He found someone to run the business, and he worked intensively with our headwaiter. That was the first time I thought the restaurant* could *have an overarching administration. He chose the restaurant's first general manager and even brought in a computer. I thought,* Oh, no! *But in the end, I loved what he did. And he loved being part of the restaurant, and in the book he later published, he wrote a whole chapter on the very unorthodox, spontaneous management of Chez Panisse. He'd never seen anything run like that before, but he really got something about Chez Panisse. He was interested in it because it was unlike anything else. He called the book* Organic Leadership.

# CHAPTER 3

# Queen of the Garden

I was born near the end of the Second World War, in 1944, so I grew up during the rise of a particular postwar culture in the United States—it was very much about a certain idea of AMERICA. We had just saved Europe, and the country was in a great economic boom—*that* was my early childhood. A lot about it was idyllic for a child like me, but only if you didn't look too closely. There was conformity, McCarthyism, the Cold War, and housewives taking little pills to survive. And, of course, there was the food. Americans had never had deep roots in gastronomy or agriculture; we didn't really eat for the pleasure of eating, and we didn't really grow food for flavor. So when big companies came in with their time-saving cooking gadgets and shortcuts, we fell for them. We were swept away. The idea was that cooking was drudgery, and these appliances helped women with the arduous work. It was billed as a sort of liberation of the housewife, and if taste was the sacrifice, so be it. That's when all these conveniences took over: electric carving knives, frozen food, blenders, TV dinners. My mother had all those things, she did—but maybe because of those conveniences, it took her a long time to become a good cook.

What I remember most about dinners—other than bickering with my sisters—is that we all sat down together at the dinner table every night at seven o'clock, and that I had to sit there until I ate everything on my plate, whether it was frozen peas or frozen lima beans, or tomato salad or corn on the cob from the garden in the summer. We'd have chicken sometimes, or steak on very special occasions—I always wanted to eat steak and green beans, that was my ideal meal. But more often we'd have a casserole with ground chuck; hotdogs with cheddar cheese and a piece of bacon; meatloaf with tomato sauce; or chop suey from a can. Oh, and iceberg lettuce salad, with a Wishbone dressing from a bottle. And frozen fish sticks! We never had bread with dinner—just baked potatoes or occasionally Uncle Ben's rice. There was no dessert regularly, except what we called "fruit cup," fruit salad from a can, with everything chopped up into a tiny dice; I'd fish out the prized maraschino cherry bits and eat them first. Sometimes I'd make banana milkshakes with my mother in the afternoon—bananas, ice, milk, and vanilla extract, blended together and poured into a tall glass—but that was it for sweets.

My mother was a health food person, even in the 1950s—that's what she spent a lot of her time learning about. In the mornings, she would listen to Carlton Fredericks, the health guru of the time, on the radio—he had a nutrition call-in program called *Design for Living*. "Health food" meant something different then: for example, bacon was a big part of it. Still, she never used margarine, that she didn't do, and there was a lot of whole milk in the house. And vitamins, vitamins, vitamins—my mother really believed in them, and I still take them to this day, although sometimes when I was little, I couldn't swallow them, and I'd spit them into my napkin when she wasn't looking. On a regular morning, we'd have eggs and bacon for breakfast, and on the weekends my father would make pancakes. We'd have grapefruit or big navel juicing oranges, and I often had a piece of brown bread toast with tons of butter and three slices of bacon—I was to have as much bacon and butter as I wanted. For my health.

I didn't like bread much as a kid, because my mother bought Pepperidge Farm brown bread. Everyone else was eating white bread then, but I didn't even like white bread so much, except for the fact that it was soft. A toasted English muffin was one of my first "Oh, I *like* that!" experiences with bread. A bakery in town made fresh plain white bread, but even that didn't hold any appeal for me. Their incredible pastries were another matter. Their jelly doughnuts were the big enticement to us after school. It was just a regular old American bakery on Main Street in downtown Chatham, with éclairs and cupcakes and jelly doughnuts. My mother probably got our birthday cakes there. The jelly doughnut was made with raspberry jam—tart inside, sugared on the outside, warm from the fryer. My friends and I devoured them before we even exited the shop, and I knew I was doing something forbidden—there was *no* telling my mom, who always said, "Sweets aren't good for you."

But my mother's health food ideas seemed to go out the window when it came to party foods. My parents had a few parties but not many. If they were having people over like my father's best friends, the Sullivers, they'd serve Fritos and dips, Wheat Thins with cheese, bread and butter pickles (I loved those), deviled eggs with paprika on top—those were the hors d'oeuvres. I liked cheddar cheese on a Ritz cracker with a bread and butter pickle—that was my ideal party food.

The big meal, the good one of the year, was Thanksgiving. There would be divine mince and pumpkin pies, wonderful stuffing, cranberry sauce, and sweet potatoes with marshmallows on top, browned in the oven. My mother wasn't a great cook, and she didn't approve of sweets, but she had a taste for pies and a real skill for making both the crust and the filling. For special occasions she made parfait pies—refrigerated custard pies with fresh strawberries or cherries.

My father had very particular tastes. He introduced me to steak and to coconut. He loved coconut cake, probably because Grandma Waters used to make a many-layered coconut cake. We always had peach ice cream and coconut cake for my dad's birthday. That was his favorite. His birthday was

August 10, when peaches were in season, so we had that flavor to celebrate. We didn't make the ice cream—my mother must have bought it—but my sisters and I did make the cake. Though even that was in the Betty Crocker white cake mix place—you added an egg and water, *et voilà*. I remember we'd bake it in a couple of cake pans, frost it with whipped cream, and scatter canned shredded coconut all over the top and sides.

*Our peach ice cream and coconut cake tradition evolved over the years into an obsession around finding the absolute best peach for my dad and making the ice cream from scratch in a hand-cranked machine, never really freezing it, just having it at that perfect texture where it's right off the dasher. And then the cake! It became a sponge cake made at Chez Panisse. We found fresh coconuts every year, cracked them, poured out the liquid, and grated the coconut flesh. Then from that fresh grated flesh, we squeezed out the coconut milk. You had to wring the cheesecloth to get one precious little half cup. We poured the coconut milk over the sponge cake—you have no idea the amount of work that went into its creation! Then we toasted the coconut, iced the cake with cream, and put the fresh toasted coconut on the outside. I'll tell you, that freshly squeezed coconut milk is so unbelievably intense and delicious and hard to produce that it later became a very special-occasion dessert at Chez Panisse. We didn't serve my dad's coconut cake, exactly, but we would pour that coconut cream onto a sponge cake layered with peaches for an incredible flavor.*

One time I went deep-sea fishing with my dad and his brother, my uncle Norman, off the Jersey coast. I caught a tuna and a flounder on the line, and they helped me pull them in. I have a picture of me in sunglasses, holding these big fish and grinning. It was the most exciting thing in my life. We brought them home, and my mother stuffed the whole fish with some sort of celery stuffing she'd read about in *Joy of Cooking*. She baked it in the oven, and I thought it was the best thing in the world, probably because I'd caught it myself.

I liked going to my friends' houses for meals most of all—the food there seemed tastier than what we had at home, and I'd eat more at other people's houses. My best friend Patsy Pill's mother made a great chili con carne, and I loved eating that at their house. They probably had plenty of garlic in that chili, though I wouldn't have been able to consciously identify it as such. At that time garlic was associated with immigrant communities and poor families—you didn't see it in the so-called traditional food of the 1950s. I don't think I ever saw a head of garlic as a child, though I did see dried, powdered garlic salt in the spice cabinet. My parents definitely didn't grow it in their garden. But I loved the foods flavored with it—even though I didn't know the garlic was responsible.

*People are always asking me, "What's your favorite vegetable?" or "What's your favorite herb or spice?" And the answer is always gar-*

*lic. I couldn't live without it. I couldn't. It's funny, because I had no childhood experience with it, and we didn't use much garlic in the beginning of the restaurant—our obsession really took off when we decided to create a festival based on the garlic harvest in 1976. Somehow we connected it with Bastille Day and decided to hold it every year on July 14—the middle of July is right when the garlic harvest is at its peak. And I think we always sort of wanted to storm the Bastille.*

*I learned so much about garlic when we started doing that festival. We went out to the fields and picked it ourselves, then watched the whole season as it changed and dried. When you're using garlic every day, you really get to know it. On the night of the first garlic festival, every dish had garlic, and people wanted to eat it in its most pure form. We roasted it and grilled it and puréed it and sautéed it—the whole nine yards. We even made garlic desserts! We did two sherbets, one with white wine and white fruits like peaches and nectarines, and another with red wine and garlic and thyme, with plums and strawberries and all the red fruits. Our chef at the time, a Frenchman named Jean-Pierre Moullé, was very skeptical about this idea, but he gamely dreamed both of those up. Were they any good? Who can say? I think we managed to pack enough sugar in there to overcome the garlic. Another intriguing garlic scheme for an early festival was to feed garlic to the mother sow of suckling pigs, so that the babies would drink garlic-infused milk; then we would roast the garlic-infused suckling pigs! We went up to the ranch and threw whole heads of garlic into the pigpen. Who knows if that infusion actually worked? But everyone loved the idea.*

Like everybody else in the country, my parents had started a vegetable garden at President Roosevelt's suggestion, as part of the war effort—they planted it very specifically to be part of that war effort, to feed themselves and other people. Even though my father considered himself a Republican, he loved Roosevelt. My mother did, too. Roosevelt was absolutely in their pantheon, so I adored him, too, and considered both him and Eleanor Roosevelt heroes—I always took on the people my mother liked. She liked to tell me about how during the war they had listened to all of FDR's fireside chats on the radio.

My dad was very civic-minded, and he was embarrassed that he couldn't be in the army during World War II because of his eyes; he was nearsighted. Instead, he became an air-raid warden in the neighborhood and did everything he could to help. So he was very diligent about the victory garden—he was pretty much in charge of it, because my mother was taking care of all the kids. I'd see him hoeing in the garden on the weekends, whenever he had free time— "idle hands are the devil's workshop" was something we heard a lot around the house.

That victory garden has certainly grown out of proportion in my memory—people think all my love of vegetables comes from it! I do think some of the fundamental taste memories of my life are from the corn and tomatoes from that garden. It was quite a significant garden, or at least it felt big to me, two lots that went all the way down to the creek behind our

My father, the air-raid warden, during World War II.

house on Passaic Avenue. It was very organized, laid out in straight rows—my father was compulsively tidy. There were tall lacy asparagus plants, tangles of red New Jersey beefsteak tomatoes, bell peppers, rhubarb, big patches of strawberries, and apple trees in the very back. When a frost was coming, my father would instruct Ellen and me to go out and put paper hats on all the tomatoes to protect them. He could be dictatorial: "Rake the leaves!" "Pull *all* the crabgrass out of the lawn!" He wanted *every* bit of crabgrass out—he was a perfectionist, and I certainly got a big dose of that from him.

As a little girl, maybe three or four years old, my mother often found me sitting in the middle of our strawberry patch when it was really hot, eating the sun-warmed strawberries. I loved being in that garden. Years later, when I was studying abroad in France, I came across an apple tree in bloom and wanted to throw myself under it and let the apple blossom petals come down on me. I felt so completely at home there and told my mother about it. She said, "When you were a baby and you were crying, I'd put you in the carriage under the mosquito netting beneath the apple trees in the backyard. And the blossoms would drift down onto the netting, and you'd stop crying right away."

In the summer of 1948, when I was four, the Chatham municipal pool held a neighborhood costume contest. Every week of the summer the pool held a different competition—a games day, an arts and crafts day—but the costume competition was the most important. My mother was clearly thrilled to have this creative outlet, and she went to town. Ellen was "Miss 1948," wearing a two-piece bathing suit covered with newspaper clippings and headlines from the year; my mother made her a newspaper hat folded like origami and a meticulously pleated newspaper skirt. Then she dressed me up as "Queen of the Garden." She harvested all sorts of fruits and vegetables from the victory garden and put them to use: she used the fernlike tops of asparagus for a big frothy skirt, and lettuce leaves became a bodice. She placed a crown of strawberries on my head, made bracelets and anklets of little red peppers, and draped pepper "ear-rings" over my ears. And I won first prize: a brand-new Kew-pie doll. I remember the shock of being called up onto the stage of the auditorium to accept my prize—I couldn't be-lieve I'd won. It was a big deal for the Waters family.

The only other competition I ever won was in third grade. We were instructed to make anything we wanted out of sundry supplies: cardboard, ribbon, construction paper, little buttons, glitter, odds and ends of fabric and bows and lace. I made a hat out of a fluted aluminum casserole tin. I edged it with lace, put a big bouquet of purple fabric violets on the side, attached ribbons so I could tie it under my neck, and set it jauntily on one side of my head. I won first or sec-ond prize for that. For many years afterward I thought, *If all else fails, I could always be a hatmaker!* Maybe that accounts for all the hats I wore for the first thirty years of Chez Panisse.

My parents always had lots of extra fruit and vegetables, and using them all up was part of the victory garden philosophy. My mother made jam from the rhubarb and applesauce from the extra apples. We gave away vegetables and traded with the Sullivers across the street, the sort of food-swapping that happens these days around community gardens. My mother was very thrifty in that way. She must have been keeping a compost heap back there in the garden, too, because we had only one little garbage can for the entire week—we were a family of six, with a garbage can only eighteen inches high and maybe twelve across. We put in a paper grocery bag, and all our trash had to fit in there. For a family of six!

At the house on Van Doren Avenue, where we moved when I was five, our garden was small by comparison—but my parents kept a vegetable garden their whole lives. We had a few roses in this garden, too, though my father was too much of a neat-as-a-pin gardener to allow the ramblers or the big old-fashioned climbers to grow. But my mother loved flowers and always pointed them out to me. I knew the names of all the flowers in our garden thanks to her. There was myrtle and little purple and white violets; lots of honeysuckle and bearded irises that had an incredible aroma; and a forsythia hedge. I'd hide beneath the forsythia hedge for hours, watching the ants walk a little trail to their anthill—it was a tiny space that was all mine, cozy and contained. On my birthday at the end of April every year, she would pick a bouquet of lilies of the valley for me. (For my fiftieth birthday, my friend Susie found every bouquet of lilies of the valley in the city of Venice and brought them to the restaurant where the celebration was—the whole place smelled like my childhood.)

In the backyard of our house were three big weeping willow trees that I loved—the branches hung low so you could creep into the tree and get hidden in there. My sisters and I used to make crowns for our heads from those flexible branches, or little chains of the English daisies that grew in the grass. My father was happy if we used the dandelions for our flower crowns, because it meant getting them out of the lawn—but then he would order us to dig out the long dandelion taproots, too (no easy task). I've never liked yellow flowers; maybe that's why.

*When Chez Panisse had been open for about fifteen years, my father saw our struggles dealing with all the different farms and getting good organic produce, and he wanted to help. "Your mother and I have time on our hands," he told me. "We could find a farmer who wants to grow specifically for Chez Panisse." The two of them went to UC Davis and asked for names of all the organic farmers within one hour of the door of Chez Panisse. They got a list of twenty or so, and over the course of six or eight months, they visited each one. They had a great time doing it. At the end, they came back, and my father made a presentation to us. "Well, we have three people in mind," he said, "but there's one farmer we like the best. He's kind of like you: he's eccentric." And he told me the story of driving up to Sobre Vista to meet Bob Cannard, and seeing beds of what looked like weeds jumbled together with wheat and God knows what—no tidy little planted rows.* What a disaster, *my father thought.*

*Then Bob took him out into the fields, pushed aside the weeds, pulled out a carrot, gave my dad a bite—it was a perfect carrot, and that was that. They had an immediate friendship, my father and Bob. There couldn't have been two more different people, but my father was sensitive enough to accept him for who he was and eventually came to treat Bob like a son. My father had the ability to take a leap of faith—to see someone far outside his own realm yet recognize his*

*tremendous talent. Bob Cannard has been growing food for Chez*
*Panisse for thirty years now. He is the exact opposite of my father:*
*he lets all the plants we once considered weeds grow—the dandelions*
*and stinging nettles and purslane—and then sells them to us! Thanks*
*to him, we make the best spring onion and wilted-nettle pizza.*

My mother's aunt, my great-aunt Ina, had big hedges of purple lilacs at her house, and I always loved the scent of them.
She would pick those lilacs and put them in vases all through
her house for the few short weeks of the year when they were
blooming. My great-aunt Ina came up frequently from Long
Branch, New Jersey, to visit us, and in the fall she and my
mother would go for rides in the woods in our old Plymouth—
we'd all go along to look at the leaves changing color. We'd do
it again in the spring and look for the pink and white flower-
ing dogwoods that were blooming. My mother and Aunt Ina
were both flower people and would tell me which plants were
which. It was a way of becoming friendly with nature.

Aunt Ina, as I've said, was the sister of the grandmother
I'd never known, my mother's mother Edna, and she had become my mother's surrogate mother after her own mother
died. Ina didn't raise my mother, but they were always very
close, and she was like a grandmother to us in a way that
Grandma Hickman never was. Aunt Ina had *great* taste in
everything and was a big influence on me; she was somebody my mother loved, loved, loved, and the two of them

were best friends. In summers, on our way to visit Grandma Hickman in Atlantic City, we would stop in Long Branch to see Aunt Ina. She had a fantastic house there, a wonderful old colonial on the Shrewsbury River.

Aunt Ina used to exclaim, "Cheroots! We're off!" Cheroots were a type of cigar she had smoked in her youth, and it was sort of a symbolic cry as we got into the Plymouth to go for a drive. She was very game: welcoming and positive, always ready for adventure. She was a big woman, quite tall, not stout but well built, with long gray hair that she pulled back and rolled up with pins, 1930s-style. When her husband, a dentist, died, she was only fifty, and she lived to be 101. For all those years she lived by herself in this ancient house where President Grant was said to have stayed once. There was a fireplace in every room, bedrooms for everybody, a beautiful inner courtyard with a wishing well in the middle, an inner porch ringing the courtyard with vines growing up, big doors out onto the alley where they used to bring the horses in, and those hedges of purple lilacs lining the property.

Ina was impressed by early Spanish architecture, and I learned later that things I assumed were antiques, like lamps and lampshades, were things she'd improvised and made herself. There was a bench next to the main fireplace that you could pull down into a table and sit on either side, nestled up near the warm fire—I loved that table. And she had little

child-size Mexican chairs for all of us girls to sit on. Above
the kitchen sink, she had arranged a whole wall with row
upon row of antique multicolored glass bottles, so it looked
like stained glass in front of you while you washed the dishes.
A corner cabinet in the kitchen was filled with beautiful
Spanish dishes she had collected—each dish was different.
And there were water and tea glasses in a rainbow of colors:
indigo, emerald green, pale rose. Aunt Ina would make orange juice and pour it into those little glasses, and we could
choose which color we wanted. I always liked the green one.

Aunt Ina didn't drink alcohol much, but she liked a little
nip every so often. Also she stood on her head every single
day until she died. She did a headstand! Every day! I remember seeing her against the wall in the mornings, in her paja-
mas, upside down. When we visited and spent the night, she

Aunt Ina with me, Laura, and Ellen in 1948.

always wanted one of the girls to stay in her bedroom with her, but I had trouble sleeping in there, listening to her snoring. I assumed that was the way of all old people: snoring, doing headstands.

Later, when I was in high school, Aunt Ina moved to Southern California and took the best of that house with her. She adapted to the California plants and landscape and made a fantastic little cactus garden there, with all different textures and shades of low-growing succulents, like a little quilt. And she had a pink peppercorn tree—we'd all sit underneath its ferny branches in the middle of her backyard. She created beauty wherever she went.

*I was lucky to be out in nature so much as a child, thanks to Aunt Ina and my mother. They showed me the beauty of the spring bulbs coming up, the fall leaves, and trees all covered with ice in winter, sparkling in the lamplight. I really believe that nature is everybody's mother—and I think our disconnection from it is the reason for so many of the problems we have now. We haven't experienced nature, neither its beauty nor its nourishment. We've been thrown into city streets and left to fend for ourselves. Beauty is a word that the fast-food culture has taken from us—we have no idea what it means anymore. They call things beautiful, and they aren't. We've been made to feel that beauty is expensive—that you can't afford it, that beautiful things are only for the people who make a lot of money: "Come on, make a ton of money so you can have beauty, too!"*

*But you can make your house beautiful no matter what. It can be about something as simple as putting colored glass bottles on the windowsill, like Aunt Ina, or lighting candles. (Then we get to lighting! Lighting is everything.) Walking into a space that's beautiful—whether it's a room in your own home or somewhere out in the world—is a huge enticement. And when something is beautiful, everybody realizes it. It's like walking into a grove of old-growth redwoods or witnessing an extraordinary sunset—there isn't one person who isn't dumbfounded. It doesn't matter what you're thinking about or who you are. You see that kind of beauty, and you're awestruck.*

*This is the thing: I don't think recognizing or creating beauty around you is a skill limited to gifted or wealthy people. Aunt Ina and my mother introduced me to nature and showed me how to recognize beauty. It's a matter of discernment and appreciation, but anybody who is educated in a certain way is able to see that beauty. The fast-food culture deprives children of seeing the beauty around them; they're not experiencing it, not touching it, not smelling it, not living it through their senses. It's about everything in life: What do you want to look at while you're washing the dishes? Can you make your own lampshade rather than buy it? What sort of rose can you plant in your garden? What herbs can you plant on your fire escape? What kind of pan do you want sitting on the stove? What kind of handle does it have?*

*This was ultimately the way I thought about the design of Chez Panisse, in particular the design of the kitchen. I wanted the kitchen to be a beautiful space, not just for the patrons but for the people who worked there. And that didn't mean spending a lot of money (because we certainly didn't have a lot of it when we started). When you don't have very much money, you have to be kind of inventive: we focused on creating orderliness to the space so it felt uncluttered and easy to access. Sometimes it just meant changing a lightbulb or framing a poster for the wall, or setting out a bowl with beautiful ingredients. Aesthetically, a beautiful work space made me feel comfortable and inspired. It shouldn't be an afterthought. The right environment around you can make whatever job you're doing pleasurable, no matter how small the task.*

I did have the sense we lived on the poor side of town when I was young. Chatham had a wealthy side and a poor side; one had a public swimming pool, and the other had private ones. But I didn't really think about rich and poor except in relation to my father's family. I was forever scrambling for money to buy a Popsicle, but I didn't feel in any way deprived. I didn't know anything other than what we had, and my parents were happy. We had enough to eat and a place to sleep and a tight family, and I had my friends. But I did know that there was a different code of behavior when we went to visit our rich aunt Marian and uncle Harry. My father's sister, my aunt Marian, had married Harry Volk, who started Union Bank. They were my rich aunt and uncle and cousins out in California, and they would send us hand-me-downs. Very definitely they were from money. In the 1950s my uncle Harry had a Chrysler Imperial luxury car that actually had a record player in it. My father was nervous around them. We had to act a certain way when we visited them in Brentwood—my parents strictly mandated that we were to behave well.

We were lower middle class—we never went out to dinner, we never bought new clothes, and my mother was pretty economical. Aunt Ina had her house, but she wasn't wealthy. Uncle Harry was in an entirely different echelon.

I don't remember if I felt bad that I couldn't get new clothes, that I had to wear my sister's. I did get a fresh pair of shoes every time I needed them. That was the one new item I was allowed—my mother believed we should all have sturdy shoes that fit us, and she would take us to shoe shops where they measured the length and width of my foot with great care. But I only wore hand-me-down clothes; every year in the fall, it was a ritual for me to climb up the attic stairs, look at the clothing racks my mother kept up there, and choose from the clothes Ellen had outgrown. Those clothes lasted way too long—they never wore out! Poor Susan.

As a child, I watched that wonderful television show where a millionaire would go knock on a door and give someone a million dollars—the show is the story of how that person spends the money. I loved that when I was little. I've always wanted to be the one either getting it or giving it. And I wish I had a million dollars so that I could give it away. I *love* to give money away. To this day, I never spend more than I think I'm going to get—if I can't imagine how

I'm going to earn it, I don't spend it. But if I can imagine it, I spend it before I even get the money. I've never kept a budget for myself, never written anything down. I've been that way for as long as I can remember—I've always spent my money before I even had it in hand.

I never felt that people treated me differently because of how much money we had or didn't have. Race separated people more than money. The city of Chatham wasn't allowed to have a movie theater because the authorities thought that meant "undesirable" people would come to town. To watch movies, we had to go to a neighboring town, Madison. It was much more about race than about class or money, though all three were linked: *undesirable* was code for *black*. There were no black kids in my school, and even somebody from Greece or Italy was deemed "undesirable." One girl, for example, who lived next to my friend Patsy Pill, was considered unusual because she came from an Italian family. I was curious about her, but we avoided playing with her. I have so much shame about it now—that from childhood we unwittingly adopted that prejudice against people. I believe that when you grow up with people who are different from you—when you're a kid and you roll around in the grass with them and eat with them at school—you have that intimate contact and innate openness forever.

We didn't have money, but we never went to fast-food restaurants. My parents knew they were cheaper, but my mother had a sense that they weren't good for us, and she felt she could cook even less expensively for us at home. The only real fast-food restaurant I ever went to was Howard Johnson—that was one of the early national chains. Howard Johnsons were known for their ice creams, and in the summers a trip there was our biggest treat: they had *all* these different flavors. This must have been in the early 1950s. My father would drive out to the Howard Johnson in Madison or Summit—it took about half an hour to get there from Chatham. We went there only for ice cream, we didn't eat anything else. I loved butterscotch and cherry vanilla, those were my flavors.

*I later found out that Jacques Pépin, somebody I greatly admire and who became a good friend, consulted for Howard Johnson when he first came to this country. Jacques came to Chez Panisse many times after it opened, and he's a teacher in the first circle; one time in the early 1980s he cooked a meal at Chez Panisse—he even illustrated and calligraphed the menu!—and we still make galettes every day in the café the way he taught us to.*

I liked ice cream from the Good Humor Man. I love that name, Good Humor Man—can you imagine? He drove down Van Doren Avenue playing that tinkling music pretty much every afternoon in the summer. When I was very young, I used to steal nickels out of my mother's purse to get ice cream—though I'm sure everyone must have known

I was stealing that money. I'd hide out on the street where my mother couldn't see me, waiting to flag down the truck for ice cream and sherbet. My favorite was a cherry lime Popsicle—one side was lime and had bits of lime peel in it, and the other side had cherry with cherry bits in it. I didn't like chocolate much then—I liked butterscotch, but not chocolate.

*When you're involved in a major philosophical discussion about food, trying to convince someone of something, you want to serve that person a food that he or she won't be able to live without. In such cases, I often pull out mulberry ice cream. Beautiful ripe ingredients are what make the difference with ice cream. After the restaurant started and we were on the hunt for the best fruits in the area, we found Charlie Grech, a farmer in Sonoma who had a gigantic ancient mulberry tree, and we started bringing the fruit from just that one tree to the restaurant. The mulberries were incredibly delicate, and the season was so short, so we always put the most perfect ones in our fruit bowl for the few weeks of the season when they were ripe. We made a syrup out of the rest of the mulberries that we could use the whole year long for ice cream. It's one of those mysterious flavors that isn't like anything else.*

*One time for an August birthday of the restaurant, we decided to give away mulberry ice-cream cones on the sidewalk out front. But I was afraid that if we just gave them away, they'd go in a half a minute, so we charged two dollars a cone. I set my daughter up with her friend to sell them—she was about eight at the time. Of course, they sold out in a minute anyway! One guy who bought a cone came up to me afterward and said, "This was the greatest thing I've ever had in my life for two dollars!" Mulberry is an ice cream that makes your jaw drop.*

During summers in New Jersey, I remember the fog machine—at least, that's what we called it, the fog machine; we loved it because it spewed out this mist, and my sisters and I would go riding after it on our bicycles so we could get lost in the fog. I remember our mother *screaming* at us to get away from it, just screaming. These were exterminators, who came almost every evening in the summer when the sun was setting, to kill mosquitoes. They really came all the time, because it was a very swampy area there. I cannot *imagine* how they sprayed pesticides like that every night, and that kids were allowed to be out there in it.

My father had a barbecue grill in the yard, and when it was warm outside, he would cook steak and pick corn from our garden and throw it all on the grill. Every summer I loved that steak and corn on the cob. My father did a lot of grilling on weekends—chicken, chops, everything. I remember him out there smoking a cigarette, carefully tending to the steaks, and turning the corn with his tongs, in a short-sleeved shirt and a spotless apron—he was fastidious like that.

My father never stopped working and was resistant to taking vacations. But one summer he had some training

to do for his job up in Maine, and we all went up to take a vacation on the coast while he was training. We stayed at an EconoLodge, and I played hide-and-seek with my sisters in the cornfields. We all liked it up in New England so much that my dad was convinced that perhaps vacations were worth it after all. Every summer after that we'd go to Squam Lake in New Hampshire. We'd go out to the beach in the evenings, make a fire, and have a clambake, dumping all the clams onto the seaweed that came with them and piling more seaweed on top.

*One time in the early years of Chez Panisse, I re-created the feeling of our Squam Lake clambake, and we cooked lobsters out in the yard behind the restaurant. Mark Miller, our chef at the time, was originally from back East, lobster territory, so he knew what he was doing. We'd never cooked over fire at that point—we didn't have a proper grill inside, so we dug out the whole backyard and lined the fire pit with rocks. Mark got live lobsters and boxes of seaweed and got a big fire going outside in the pit. He heated everything up really, really hot, put the live lobsters right on the kelp, covered it with yet more seaweed, and then put a giant pot on top. I can't believe we did this in the backyard and served them in the dining room that night! There was so much steam and smoke that I was afraid the fire department would show up, but those lobsters were delicious— they absorbed all the flavors of the wood, and they were so perfectly cooked, steamed with that briny seaweed and the aromatic wood underneath. I've always wanted to make lobster like that again, but you need a whole lot of seaweed and a whole lot of know-how.*

On Squam Lake we had a little rowboat with an outboard motor that my father named the *SALEM C.*—for Susan, Alice, Laura, Ellen, Margaret, and Charles. We'd take the boat out to the Yard Islands, in the middle of the lake, to collect tiny wild blueberries. When we'd bring them back to the house, my father would make us wild blueberry pancakes. We played our first games of Scrabble out there, too—it was invented around then. One year Susan and Laura had chicken pox and couldn't run around, so we all sat out on the huge wraparound porch and played Scrabble. It was one of the rare times when all four girls played together—we didn't have much choice of playmates up there, of course, but the four of us had fun at Squam Lake, picking wild blue-berries and climbing Mount Chocorua, out there in nature together. Many years later I recognized Squam Lake in the film *On Golden Pond* right away: that nostalgic setting with the rowboats, the sunsets over the lake, the pine trees, the sandy beaches, the quiet.

**★★★★**
**FINAL**

# DAILY ◉ NEWS

Copr. 1951 by News Syndicate Co. Inc. NEW YORK'S PICTURE NEWSPAPER   Trade-Mark Reg. U. S. Pat. Off.

**3¢**

Vol. 32.  No. 245        New York 17, Friday, April 6, 1951★        84 Main+4 Manhattan Pages        3 Cents

# A-SPY COUPLE
# DOOMED TO DIE

Story on Page 2

## Use Chiang's Army, Mac Asks

Story on Page 2

**On Way to Chair.** Gloved hands folded, Mrs. Ethel Rosenberg, 35, rides in rear of prison van on way to Women's House of Detention. Julius Rosenberg, 32, is separated from his wife by wire screen in van outside U. S. Courthouse. They were sentenced to death for passing A-bomb secrets to Reds, enabling Russia to perfect bomb ahead of schedule.    —Story p. 2

## CHAPTER 4

# When the Tide Rushes In

When it comes to sleep, you really remember only the bad times. In the summer when I was young, I was always too hot and had mosquito bites all over, and I would toss and turn. I've always been a sensitive sleeper—at a slumber party, I'd stake out my pillow and blanket first and always take the most comfortable bed. I had lots of nightmares when I was a child. For seven years, I had a recurring nightmare— it started in the early 1950s, when the Rosenbergs were executed. A house a couple doors away from ours was always dark, and the woman who lived there never handed out Halloween candy. I dreamed that she would pull me into the house, take me out to the backyard, and put me in an electric chair. In the dream, a big electric robot would pick me up and put me down in the chair, and I'd wake up screaming. I had that dream for years and years. My mother would have to come in and pat me on my stomach to help me go back to sleep.

It was a very fearful time. When we were little, we had air-raid alerts at school and would have to practice what to do in case there was an atomic bomb. We had to hide under our desks, or go down into the basement hallways of the school and sit against the walls with our hands on top of our heads until the bell stopped ringing.

God knows everyone in the 1950s was in denial about everything that was going on. Not just politically—there was no discussion about *anything*: who had lost a job, who was having an affair with whom, who was unhappy. We never talked as a family about anything personal. Not ever. Least of all anything to do with sex or the body. We took baths together as very young kids, but that was it; you dressed in the bathroom, with the door closed. It was a pretty puritanical upbringing. My mother was a radical in some ways, but sexual repression was in the air when we were young. My mother wasn't imposing it on us consciously, but she was clearly uncomfortable with sex herself, so that discomfort was passed along to us. It was a pattern of behavior for almost all families then.

When I was four, my sister Laura was born, and I remember looking into a room and finding my mother nursing her. I was absolutely shocked—breast-feeding was something you didn't see in the 1950s. You either gave the baby formula or you went someplace very private to nurse the baby. And my mother *was* somewhere private, she was in her bedroom—but I just peeked in. I was stunned to see that and incredibly jealous; I was sure that it meant my mother liked Laura better than me.

On one of those trips up to Squam Lake, my parents befriended the Monleys, a couple in the cabin next door. They were big drinkers, and my father was glad for an excuse to start happy hour early. So my parents needed sitters to watch us kids down by the water's edge while they were having their happy hour—or happy hours—over at the Monleys'. One year when I was about ten, a teenage girl from around the lake would come over to watch us. I was mesmerized by this buxom babysitter's body. I told her she was so beautiful and maybe even asked to touch her bodice. She scolded me severely, and I was deeply ashamed—she made me feel like I was dirty. I was skinny as a rail at the time, wearing big shorts with my tiny knobby knees sticking out. I had braces and brown hair with heavy blunt bangs, like Buster Brown. And here was this beautiful, shapely older girl I admired so much, shaming me.

I entered puberty when I was in seventh grade. I was on my way to school, wearing white suede shoes and socks, and my white crinolines and a pink skirt with flowers. I fled straight home again in horror. I'd never spoken to my mother or Ellen or anyone about that stuff, but I knew that *this* was that terrible thing that happened to girls—the Curse, that's what we called it. My God, it was distressing. My mother got a slim, clinical book for me that explained what it was all about and left it under my pillow—that constituted our whole discussion. Even today it feels embarrassing to talk about—I can't even say those words, not even after Eve Ensler.

I was so unaccustomed to talking about anything sexual with my mother and father that decades later, when I was pregnant at thirty-eight, I felt uncomfortable that my mother would actually know, once and for all, that I had had sex. I was so ashamed. Of course, when I did tell her I was pregnant, all she said was, "How wonderful, Alice! How wonderful." She was enthusiastic, like it was the greatest gift. My father, too. And here I was, embarrassed because Stephen, the man I was living with, and I weren't married yet. I was worrying because she'd think we "did it"! The shame! It's hilarious, but that's how deep it was. I never talked to my sisters about crushes—nothing. Later on in high school, I drank a lot, and I think a large part of it was drinking to feel free.

The first person who had a crush on me was Richie Thomas, when I was in sixth or seventh grade. Richie would write me anonymous notes, signing them "from your secret admirer, TR"—he flipped his initials around. (Clever!) Even though we became friends in school, somehow I never figured out he had sent those notes until later, after I left Chatham. Richie Thomas had amazing handwriting and was a great writer. We kept in touch even after I moved from Chatham to Michigan City, Indiana—he was the one person I kept up with from my grammar school days.

After ninth grade, we moved to Michigan City, and I have no memory of the move except that I hated leaving Chatham. I couldn't believe I had to leave. By that time Ellen had gone off to college, so it was just Laura, Susan, and me—I felt like I was being dragged along with the little kids of the family. Right before we left, I was out on the soccer field, playing for our high school team. I was always the shortest in the class and very small to be out there among all these big senior women. During the game, someone kicked the ball hard at me, hard enough that it really hurt, and knocked me down. And I thought for the first time, *Well, fine, I'm* glad *I'm leaving.*

My father had worked for the Prudential in Newark, and they transferred him out to work in Chicago—but we would live in Michigan City, sixty miles from Chicago and just five blocks from the beach of Lake Michigan. The house was at Stop 27 of the bus line, with big trees all around, in a nice old neighborhood. The reason my father tolerated the hour-and-a-half commute was that my mother loved the beach so much—he knew the move had been hard on her, and he wanted to be considerate.

I liked the beauty of Michigan City's winding streets, and the beach. I especially loved the Catholic church there, being inside and looking up and feeling awed, though no one in the family was particularly religious, least of all me. I've always been attracted to sacred spaces—I think everybody is.

I needed a summer job, so the first summer we were in Michigan City, I was a carhop at the Country Cousin—my first job ever, and my first in a restaurant. I thought it would be an easy job to get and figured maybe I could get some good food there for free, because I still wasn't crazy about the food my mother made at home. As a carhop at the Country Cousin, I waited on cars on roller skates, serving fried chicken and honey and biscuits and Coca-Cola in glasses—wearing a checkered top and a straw hat, like a country girl. The hat might have even had little pigtails attached. People *really* liked the food there—and so did I.

Another summer I worked in Michigan City at Winski & Winski Enterprises, a hotdog stand in the Jewish part of the beach—everything in Michigan City was segregated that way. Two brothers ran it, and I probably got the job because of my vast Country Cousin experience. I thought the brothers were cute. I didn't work there very long—maybe I even quit—but apparently the Winski brothers remembered me, because they wrote to me not long ago and sent me a picture of their hotdog stand.

Shortly after I arrived, I joined the cheerleading squad at school. I was an extrovert—I was trying to find my way into my new school, and I thought maybe that would be the route to making friends. Plus, I was good at cartwheels. I don't think I was a cheerleader for a very long time—perhaps I was even just filling in as a sub, or maybe I quit. But I absolutely remember the cheer we sang: "Good, better, best! Never let it rest! Till the good is better, and the better is best!" I suppose that's my motto still.

At school I made friends with Dana McDermott, a very beautiful, buxom, and sensuous-looking girl with thick wavy black hair. Her mother was Italian, and her father was Irish. Her father was sharp-tempered and always insisted that Dana had to be home at a certain time—probably to keep the amorous high school boys at bay—and she was scared of him. But strict father aside, I loved going to Dana's house, especially when her mother was pulling bread out of the oven. It was neither brown nor precisely white but sort of a rustic Italian bread. We wanted to eat it while it was still hot from the oven so the butter would melt. I'd always ask Dana, "Is your mom baking bread today?"

*There are few things as perfect as delicious, real, freshly baked bread. It's universally loved: the aroma, the taste, the look. At the very beginning of Chez Panisse, we bought sourdough—San Francisco sourdough was what everyone ate then, a very Italian bread. But I was dissatisfied with it. I wanted French bread, since we were a French restaurant, and I wanted it to be fresh when people tasted it.*

*Steve Sullivan started at Chez Panisse when he was sixteen. He began as a busboy—he was in high school and first came to us for a summer, then kept working at the restaurant while he was going to UC Berkeley. Steve saw our need for bread—I was always complaining about the Italian sourdough, wanting the real thing. So he started making loaves in his dorm room and would bring them in for us to taste. There was a lot of "No, this doesn't work," or "No, not like this," and then one day he brought a loaf in, and it was like "You're on!" It was great, because we were fine-tuning and tasting breads over and over again for a really long time, but he respected all of us and took all that calibrating in the right spirit. And then he hit on it exactly, and the result was delicious. Steve went on to bake all his bread at the restaurant, running upstairs and downstairs, misting water on loaves. Eventually he started his own place, Acme Bread Company, because he was driving us crazy dominating the ovens. We've been happily getting our bread from him ever since.*

I didn't see much of Laura and Susan in the Michigan City years—my mother was still making dinner for all of us, but I was rarely at home anymore. Being at the table at seven p.m. went out the window, because my father was getting home quite late, eating his dinner after all of us, and I was in a whole different world in high school. Michigan City High was gigantic. And it was tracked, so students were divided up by grade-point average. Our school was 80 percent black and 20 percent white, yet I never saw a black student in any of my classes. This was a school that banned *The Grapes of Wrath*—that's the sort of place it was. It was all about sports and the basketball team. I didn't spend much time doing homework, though I stayed after school for algebra tutoring with my poor math teacher. He pulled me through that class and finally gave me a good old B. But not because I really learned algebra. I think he just felt sorry for me.

. . .

I drank a lot of hard liquor in high school—I'd never really drunk wine or alcohol but jumped right into the hardest stuff. It knocked me out—it made me sexually loose and comfortable with people, all that stuff that hard liquor does. In Indiana it was Seagram's and 7-Up—the boys always had it. It's lucky I'm alive today; in the middle of the night, I'd take the keys from my mother's purse and climb out the back window. Then my pals and I would push my parents' car out the driveway, and we'd drive it in the snow drinking Seagram's. I can't believe that we did that. And I can't believe my parents didn't know. And there were the "make-out parties." I'd have ten or fifteen boys and girls over—more boys than girls—and we'd cram into our basement and sit on the couch and just kiss. We'd drink and play music and dance to all the rock 'n' roll of the late 1950s: Buddy Holly, the Everly Brothers . . . I know every word of all those songs. I especially know the slow ones because I liked to dance with the boys to the slow ones. Romantic music was my favorite—ballads, that sort of thing. I still know all the words to every song Johnny Mathis ever sang. Another song I loved was the Platters' version of "Ebb Tide" with all those dreamy lines about the tide rushing in and out. My sister Laura told me recently that when I had a party, my mother would take Laura and Susan and hide in the bathroom, because it got so wild they were afraid to come out!

Getting men to pay attention to me was a big part of high

school. At a store in town called the Lady's Shop, I'd linger over the mannequins in the windows, slender and alluring, imagining myself dressed like that. They had tight cashmere sweaters and long, fitted wool skirts that matched, in soft pinks and yellows and baby blues, all pastels; and Capezio ballet flats with leather polka dots sewn on, little pink and pale blue spots. I had to save up for these outfits because the shop wasn't cheap. But I wanted men to be interested in me, and I knew the way I dressed was part of that. These clothes felt very sophisticated, very soft and feminine and shapely.

I never thought of myself as being pretty when I was little, though I loved the dresses Aunt Doris made for me and felt pretty in them. I had been much more of a tomboy when I was younger, and it wasn't until I was a teenager that I started going *Oh!* and being completely aware of how I looked. Sex and beauty get mixed up, and when people find you attractive, then you start to think, *Hmm, then maybe I must be.* When I look at pictures of me from around then, like a picture of me on a beach in my strapless checkered bathing suit—it's funny, I was always worried about being pretty, but maybe I also took it for granted. As I grew up, I realized I had some kind of sex appeal, but that might have come from my great interest in it—maybe I was so *interested* in it that they just couldn't resist.

My first boyfriend in Michigan City was Tommy Wojcinski. I liked him because he had a Pontiac convertible. And then there were John Gill, Leroy Wolfert, and Bill

Finn. Leroy Wolfert was kind of a hood, and Bill Finn was a rich kid who lived in a house up on a hill. I don't remember having a curfew—I was probably supposed to be home at a certain time, but I never made it. In the summers I went waterskiing on Lake Michigan and met every guy who had a boat. All the rich families summered on the lake. John Daley, Mayor Daley's son, took me waterskiing. His family had a summer home along the lake near us. After waterskiing, we'd get one of his parents' limousines to drive us into Chicago, and we'd eat on Rush Street, at one of the expensive restaurants there. We'd go to the Pump Room—that was in the days of the flaming shish kebab. The Pump Room was fancy, bordering on garish: the uniformed doorman who opened the door of the limo, the dark wood, the big round red leather booths we would slide into. We had a sort of privilege there, because John was the mayor's son.

I was conscious that John and Bill were rich and I wasn't. These guys were around just for the summer and were all off to military academies in the fall. Michigan City was dramatically segregated between races, religions, neighborhoods, but I didn't feel pigeonholed at all. I didn't have the religion thing, and our family wasn't rich, but we weren't exactly poor, either, so I felt comfortable moving around in that whole world, through different groups.

On those excursions to the Pump Room, or driving around in the snow drinking Seagram's and 7-Up, I was often the only girl in a car with two or three boys. I liked hanging out with a whole lot of guys, I did. My mother didn't know about any of that—I just made up stories, and she didn't interrogate me for details. And my father was commuting an hour and a half to and from Chicago every day, so he wasn't around to ask hard-hitting questions. My parents were always hands-off. It's not that they didn't care, they *really* cared, but there was a loving kind of willful ignorance on their parts. My parents didn't put it all together simply because they didn't want to know. I thought of it as a little like *What they don't know won't hurt them.*

One summer I met a friend of Bill Finn's—Bill was a friend of mine, but it was hard to tell between the boyfriends and the friends sometimes. This friend of Bill's was slender and blond and handsome, with a southern accent—he was from Shreveport, Louisiana—and terribly polite, opening the doors, saying "Yes, ma'am," all that. I completely fell for him. I had a little summer affair with him, and then in the fall he went away to Culver Military Academy and wrote me beautiful letters—he had wonderful handwriting. This boy invited me down to Culver, a couple hours away, to their big formal military ball; he was a senior, about to graduate, and I was younger, maybe still a sophomore. Everyone knew I was going down for the ball, and I'd been planning and getting my clothes together for weeks: a fancy yellow lace dress that belled out from the waist.

I caught a ride down to his school and met him out by the lake on campus. I was wearing my lace dress, and he brought me three white gardenias for my wrist. I was intoxicated—he was in his white uniform, I was wearing these gardenias, and I was enraptured by the beauty and the romance of it all. That whole night was a total fantasy, dancing the slow dances with him. I didn't have girlfriends there with me; I was alone.

Strangely, I didn't understand this boy's intentions, though I should have guessed. Even though I was a little wild, with the make-out parties and the heavy groping in the backs of cars, I'd never gone all the way. But after this dance, he wanted exactly what you would think he wanted. He was definitely drinking, and I suspect we both were. He got really rough with me. In the end, what he wanted didn't come to pass, but I was so shocked, I was crying—he'd tried to take me by force. The letters and the dancing had been such romantic foreplay, and then here we were in this back room someplace, and I felt like *I didn't bargain for this*. Nobody had ever pushed me before like that, and I couldn't believe someone so charming and civil and gallant would try to do that.

I don't know how I got home—I vaguely remember being asleep in someone's car afterward. I was appalled, though. I'd thought he was so polite and southern. I used drinking as a way to loosen myself up and go with everything—and I certainly enjoyed flirting. But playing with that power of sexuality, you just don't know how far it's going to go. It went from being this beautiful moment by the lake with gardenias to just—*oh my God*. I never saw him again, and I didn't tell my sisters or anyone about it.

*In the mid-1970s when I was living in Berkeley, someone broke into my apartment in the night and tried to rape me. I was living behind my friend's house in a little garage space, with my bed in a second-story loft. When I came home that night, I'm sure I locked the door as usual. I went to bed and woke up in the middle of the night with somebody's hand clamped over my mouth in the darkness. The man signaled for me to turn around so I couldn't see him, and he made me go down the steps to get money. As soon as he let go of my mouth for a second, I started screaming bloody murder. But he was standing right behind me and grabbed my throat so hard that I passed out.*

*When I came to, he was still there. I said I didn't have any money, but I'd get him whatever he needed. I had a restaurant, we could go there, it wasn't far—I was talking as fast as I could, and he covered my mouth again. He'd dropped his knife somewhere in the house and had to find it, so we were walking around in the dark with his hand on my mouth. He made me go up the stairs to the loft where the bed was.*

*He found his knife and pushed me onto the bed. Before he could do anything, though, I leaped headfirst out the window. He held on to my leg for a few seconds but dropped me. Fortunately it was only eight feet down to the lawn. I never stopped screaming from the moment I got free. Someone called the police, but by the time they arrived, he'd already gone.*

*The police gave me a big book of potential suspects to look through, and even though there was no way I could tell what he looked like in the darkness, I flipped through it anyway. The most horrifying part was that, in this book with hundreds of pages of convicted rapists, each man would go to jail for only about three months, and then he'd be let out again. A rapist from the neighborhood had recently been released, so the police assumed it had been him; he must have got into my house before I came home, and he'd been there the whole time while I got ready for bed. Afterward I moved and put dead bolts on all my doors and locks on my windows. I was uncomfortable sleeping by myself for a long time.*

*Oddly enough, it didn't affect my passion for men. I had a new sense of my physical weakness in that circumstance, and I was terrified that someone might break into my house. But my fear absolutely did not extend to all men. It was about power and violence, not about all men.*

*You never really know what your reaction is going to be in a scenario like that: if you'll freeze with terror, be silent, or go limp. I'd always thought I'd rather give in completely than be killed; I'd rather be raped than dead. But after this happened, I realized it was the other way around—I'd rather be dead than raped. Rape is such a violation, and I was prepared to do everything I could to stop him. I mean, I jumped out of a second-story window. The whole experience shocked me, but I also couldn't believe I had that resistance in me, that I was willing to risk my life to keep that from happening. I never, ever imagined that. In the end, I felt empowered because I'd been able to think of a way out.*

# CHAPTER 5

# From the Beach to Berkeley

My father was very successful in his job as a human resources psychologist in Chicago—the Prudential insurance company thought he was working miracles. In 1961, the summer before my senior year in high school, he was promoted to a senior position within the company, this time in Los Angeles. Everybody in the family was upset; it would be a big move. The only one who could find any redeeming value in it was my mother, because Aunt Ina had moved out to San Diego a few years before, and we would be living close to her again. But I was absolutely unwilling to go.

In the weeks before we were to leave, though, I became convinced I was pregnant. When you've been drunk in the backseats of cars, you're really not sure what happened after the fact. I was terrified. I tried all the old wives' remedies, drinking green teas, everything. Days before we were to leave for California, I found out I wasn't pregnant after all—and I was *so* happy and relieved to board the plane and

leave everything behind. I just thought, *Thank God*. I felt I
was lucky to get out of there unscathed.

Ellen was with us that summer, home from college, so
on our way out to California, we took a family road trip. We
flew from Michigan City to Denver, then all four girls packed
into a car, in our big circle skirts we always wore with the
crinolines underneath, barely fitting into the backseat. We
toured around to the Garden of the Gods, Yellowstone, and
the salt flats near Salt Lake City, where my mother's younger
brother, our uncle Fred, was working for the army at Dugway
Proving Ground. We finally got to Los Angeles, then drove
and drove and drove to get to our new home, and I thought,
*What awful place is this?* Everything about Los Angeles in 1961
put me off—it was all palm trees and cars and freeways. The
houses in Beverly Hills had spotlights as if they were on a
movie set—it wasn't even Christmastime. I thought the entire city was gaudy. My parents had found a house on top of
a hill in Sherman Oaks, overlooking the city. It was one of
those contemporary tract homes and didn't have much of a
garden—though my father tried to plant a small one there. I
was offended by L.A. and just wanted to leave.

My senior year at Van Nuys High School was weird. They
thought I must be quite smart, because I'd got nearly all A's
at Michigan City High School, and I was in the National
Honors Society. So I was dropped into the advanced place-
ment classes along with this very academically competitive
crowd of other seniors, and I think my sudden presence in

their final year must have aroused their curiosity about my academic abilities. In English class, the teacher asked us to write a short essay on something we knew really well. So I, of course, wrote about waterskiing. The teacher asked me to read my paper aloud in front of the class, and as I started to read, I suddenly became completely self-conscious, having an excruciating realization that I didn't know anything at all, that I'd written this terribly foolish paper. I was so nervous reading it, I could barely speak. I sat down once I finished, and the boy behind me, a tall, dark-haired boy who was president of the student body and articulate and well spoken, said, "And *what* language were you speaking that in?"

I don't think the teacher had asked me to stand up out of sadism—maybe he'd found the details in my essay interesting, or even its naïveté! I'll never know. But that boy's comment made me so ashamed. I cried at my desk, as if it were the worst thing that could ever happen. I felt I was just not smart enough. And that feeling was so shocking that I've never recovered. (I also became determined to get that boy to fall in love with me.) I'm still intimidated and reverential around people who are smart and have been educated. It's taken me a long, long time to feel like I can speak in my own words.

Like Michigan City High School, Van Nuys High School was huge. But Michigan City was several floors high, while Van Nuys was this sprawling, charmless structure—just like the city around it. Los Angeles felt endless to me. I lived there only a year, so I didn't really get to know the culture at all. But I made some interesting friends at Van Nuys who were all really smart, which is funny considering my insecurities in that department: Louise Brandt, John Boros, Paul Goldman, and Eleanor Bertino.

Eleanor ended up becoming my friend for life. She was elegant and tall, Italian, with beautiful skin. I'd go to her house in the valley sometimes; her father was a cartoonist for Walt Disney, and her mother was from Tuscany, a really good cook who made northern Italian dishes and always had a little wine with dinner, which was practically unheard of at the time. (Years later, after Chez Panisse had been open for quite some time, Eleanor brought her mother to the restaurant, and we served them a radicchio salad. Her mother's response: "Oh, that awful stuff my father used to grow. I didn't think I'd have to eat it again.") Eleanor's mother had a Tuscan sense of fashion and worked in the credit department at Bullock's department store, so Eleanor knew how to shop—she was always very well dressed. I appreciated most of all, though, that Eleanor seemed to look out for me somehow—she had poise and confidence and was like a big sister to me.

I didn't date anyone seriously at Van Nuys because I was new, thrown in with this intellectual crowd. I did eventually get the student body president—the one who made that cutting remark after my waterskiing essay—to take me out on a date or two, but I couldn't get him to kiss me. I really couldn't fathom that this boy cared about other things besides sex. I mean, he read books! I volunteered to be part of his project that sent books to Kenya, and I was determined to get more books than anyone else to impress him. But with the group of people I met there, dating wasn't the focus, and they were simply not interested in me in that way. I couldn't *believe* I couldn't seduce this boy. Mind you, I tried—I was doing my best to seduce them all. Seduction was my modus operandi—and it had been rather successful in Michigan City. The kids here also didn't drink as much as those in Michigan City. It was just different.

Thinking about college, I wanted to go to Middlebury, in Vermont. We had visited there when Ellen was looking at colleges, and I thought Middlebury was the most beautiful school—New England steeples, green lawns, big trees—and I liked that it specialized in languages, which gave it an international air. (Never mind that I'd never studied a foreign language, other than a bit of Latin in fourth grade.) But my parents said I couldn't apply—I had to choose from only the UC schools, because they cost ninety-eight dollars a semester for California residents. We drove around to all the campuses—Berkeley and Santa Barbara and Riverside and UCLA. Eleanor was going to Santa Barbara, so I decided to go there, too. A little group of us were going there, and that was that.

UC Santa Barbara was a new campus, all low buildings, nothing dramatic or beautiful. It didn't quite feel like a university.

The campus was perched on a cliff overlooking the ocean, and I could look out the windows of my classrooms and see sand and waves down below. And that meant the rhythms of the school had a certain casualness. I would watch guys carrying their surfboards past us on their way down to the beach. The weather was almost always warm, which felt like an invitation to skip class. So we'd get bottles of wine, walk down to the beach, and make out with boys. (Other girls would go into the water, but I never did—it was way too cold for me.)

As soon as I got to college, I saw it was a whole different scene from Van Nuys—going to parties, doing all that Santa Barbara stuff. I drank too much, for sure. I'd wake up in a place and not remember how I'd got there. UC Santa Barbara had a party school reputation, and I think I knew a bit of that before I arrived. I had the feeling there was no *there* there at the university—even the city of Santa Barbara was a half hour away—and there didn't seem to be much to do other than make out at the beach.

The first semester we were in dorms. We'd had to complete a survey to identify what kind of roommate we'd like to have. I don't know what I wrote, but I was paired with somebody strange and dark and really smart, a very serious, focused girl who wore all black clothes—exactly the opposite of me. I wish I could say she had a sobering influence on me, but it was like we spoke two different languages. I'm guessing she didn't care much for everyone's beach antics.

At some point in those first few months, Eleanor convinced me we should rush for Alpha Phi. Eleanor was maybe a little more proper than me, and I suspect she thought the sorority would be a good influence for both of us and maybe help straighten me out. I don't remember how we got into Alpha Phi, but we managed it somehow. I can't say it straightened me out, though.

Alpha Phi sorority Mardi Gras costume party, circa 1963.
Front row left is Eleanor.

One course I took at Santa Barbara was on comparative religion. I loved the teacher, and I loved reading about Buddhism. So on the one hand I was learning about Buddhism, and on the other I was partying. I distinctly remember going to that class, but that's the only one.

Back home for summer vacation, I worked at the Tea Room inside the Bullock's department store in Sherman Oaks, about ten minutes from our house. It was an upscale, sophisticated restaurant where they had fashion shows at lunchtime. Eleanor got me the job; because her mother worked at Bullock's, Eleanor had worked in the kitchen at the Tea Room the previous summer. So now the two of us did it together—we were both waitresses, but we'd fill in in the kitchen every so often, since it was a small place.

I wore all white—that was my uniform in the kitchen. I thought it was much more interesting to be in the kitchen than in the dining room. Everything was made in-house—there was even a baker on staff—and the food was very good. The cooks would roast whole turkeys every day, then make turkey sandwiches and "chicken" salad sandwiches. There was a crab sandwich on the menu, too, and we helped to pick the crabs for it. The baker baked an excellent cheddar cheese bread, and we made a bacon and avocado sandwich on the toasted cheese bread—I remember the taste of that sandwich very clearly.

The Tea Room was run by Mrs. Wandra, a stocky, gray-haired woman, imposing and formidable but not unkind.

She was very particular and ran a tight ship. Her husband was an invalid, so she supported the whole family and worked tirelessly—she really knew how to run a business. She taught me some good lessons about cleaning up after service, putting all your ingredients in little cups, and keeping everything neat and ordered.

Eleanor and I worked at Mrs. Wandra's during the day, then went out, sometimes, to the Hollywood Bowl to sit in my rich uncle Harry's box to hear classical music—which Uncle Harry must not have liked. I loved classical music. We heard incredible symphonies and conductors—like Zubin Mehta, the conductor of the Los Angeles Philharmonic. We'd take some roast chicken and salad and a bottle of wine and bring our guy friends from Van Nuys who were interested in music.

Halfway through my sophomore year, I was thrown out of the sorority, Alpha Phi, for drinking—or "morals charges," that's what they called it. I'd get too drunk and lose track of time or pass out and then get home too late; Alpha Phi had strict curfews. And sometimes they'd catch me making toast or BLTs in the sorority after hours, when I wasn't supposed to be there—I certainly wasn't making them with the precision that Mrs. Wandra had taught.

I probably wouldn't have joined that sorority in the first place, except Eleanor had wanted me to. The whole system was ridiculous. Eleanor had once been called in before a grim tribunal of house mothers and alumnae because a "dark man" had picked her up in a car. They wanted to question her about this unsavory person she had been seen with. It turned out he was a Saudi Arabian prince, and he had picked Eleanor up in a beige Jaguar XKE. Another time a friend of ours in Alpha Phi, Betsy Danch, wanted to bring a girl she liked named Lucky Pearl into the sorority. Lucky's mother was a card dealer in Las Vegas. But three sorority sisters "bonged" her because of that—they signaled they were refusing to accept her just by sounding a gong, without explanation. We were disgusted by the racism and classism of it all.

Eleanor didn't want to be part of the sorority after I was thrown out. She and Betsy and our friend Sara Flanders were all bored to death at Santa Barbara anyway, so Eleanor said, "Let's just get out of here." She convinced us to transfer to Berkeley midway through the year. Berkeley was a bigger campus and was so different from Santa Barbara, with a very diverse student population. That year, 1963, was the year of the March on Washington—it happened in late August, right as we were starting classes—and later that fall Kennedy was assassinated. I was in class looking out the window through half-drawn curtains that November day when the news came over the loudspeaker that the president had been killed. I burst into tears. Everyone did. I haven't got over it yet. Terrible things were happening in the world, and the culture at Santa Barbara felt so willfully blind to the political unrest. There were rumblings about student protests, people standing up for civil rights at Berkeley. We knew something big was happening. Thank goodness Eleanor brought me with her.

At around the same time, my father was fired from his job at the Prudential—after nearly three decades with the company, one year before his pension was vested. He was doing something radical: he was encouraging employees in the company to speak up for themselves, and trying to help them organize, so he was let go. It was brutal. I was distracted at the time because I was away at college, but I remember he was crushed. He hid it, but he was devastated. He didn't want to show his face around the house. My mother was devastated, too, but terribly sympathetic. When, a few years later, he was offered a good full-time job at the University of Michigan, she was willing to make the move, even though it meant yet another cross-country relocation for her—because she knew how much my father needed to remake himself.

Berkeley in January 1964 was a complete shock. Eleanor and Sara and Betsy, who were going to be my roommates, had much more courage around the move and about being there. I remember going to a party on the upper levels of a building on Telegraph Avenue, above a bookstore—Moe's Books, I think. And I looked into this room and saw people lying on the couches, draped all over, smoking God knows what, doing God knows what drugs. I felt a little shaken.

I'd never smoked dope. I didn't understand what was going on in the room—it looked alien to me and, quite honestly, scary. Like, *Have I made the right decision?*

When I first got to the university, I was pretty overwhelmed, trying to figure out my classes. I sought out the most charismatic teachers and professors. I found one who taught a class on Beethoven's symphonies; then I took a whole course on Berlioz. I took a class on Renaissance art, and one on astronomy. It didn't matter what they were teaching as long as they had charisma. My classes were so all over the place, I could never define my major.

Sara, Eleanor, Betsy, and I had found a practical apartment on Parker Street, along with another Santa Barbara transfer, Marilyn Longinotti. It was a modern flat, a few blocks from what would later be People's Park. I thought the Berkeley campus was pretty: all the redwood trees down by Strawberry Creek, the green Beaux Arts arch over Sather Gate, the old buildings. After my classes every day, I walked out through Sather Gate, crossed Sproul Plaza, and went down Telegraph Avenue to go back to our apartment. (A couple years later, when Top Dog opened, I'd stop in there for food on my walk home. They had great bratwurst dogs from Saag's, hot buns, grilled onions, and good sauerkraut. I liked their chili cheese dog, and I loved the revolutionary feel to this little hotdog place.) A lot of coffee shops lined Telegraph, and whenever I walked past them, they were filled with people in heated conversation. Ideas were important to these people: everyone seemed to be speaking emphatically, locked in deep political debate. Students at Berkeley were a coffeehouse crowd with a beatnik urban sophistication, carrying big book bags, very somber and intense. They looked like the 1950s gone to seed—men were still wearing jackets and women were in skirts, but somehow it felt *different*. And it was much more academically rigorous. It wasn't laid-back like Santa Barbara—I mean, we had gone from the beach to Berkeley!

At Santa Barbara I'd felt a little radical, but at Berkeley I realized I wasn't at all. So much more was going on politically than I was even aware of. Berkeley had something electric, a current of activity that I was taking in—though I didn't know what the result was going to be. UC Berkeley intimidated me. I worried about the academic expectations the university had of me, worried that I hadn't studied enough, worried that it was going to be a repeat of that humiliating experience I'd had at Van Nuys with the class president—multiplied by the whole student population. I even got a tutor for some of my classes, I was so concerned. I felt I didn't know the facts, and these people were *engaged*.

Sproul Plaza was where you got the news every day. All these tables from different political organizations were set up at the entrance of Sproul Plaza, just as you walked onto campus. You walked through the plaza as you were coming back from class, and you were instantly part of what was happening, grabbing leaflets from students, listening to the

talk about showing up at noon the next day for whatever political rally was being held. Eleanor and Sara and I really liked all the tables out there—it was the exact opposite of Santa Barbara. Even though we weren't politically involved when we arrived, we were happy that there was some ferment, some interest from students in the larger world.

The Free Speech Movement started in earnest in the fall of 1964. People were voicing their anger and frustration with the war, civil rights, the political and social culture at large—but the board of regents, which ran the whole University of California system, was very clear that it wouldn't tolerate anyone challenging the status quo. At that time, all

UC faculty had to sign a restrictive "loyalty oath" in order to teach, and if what they said veered from the oath, or if they refused to sign it, they'd be fired. In the early fall of 1964, the dean of the university ruled that all the political tables at the edge of Sproul Plaza, where we got our news about the world, were banned. All political activity and fund-raising on campus were banned. If a student stood up on campus to speak out about Vietnam, they'd be dragged off by the university police.

One day in early October, I was on campus when the cops pulled up to Sproul Plaza in a car to arrest a student, Jack Weinberg, who was running the table for the Congress of Racial Equality (CORE), which had organized the Freedom Rides through the South and recruited students for civil rights demonstrations. The police dragged Jack Weinberg into the car, and then thousands of students spontaneously surrounded the car and wouldn't let it leave. Mario Savio, a senior at Berkeley, had just come back from CORE's Freedom Summer project in Mississippi, where he had been helping to register black voters. I watched him climb on top of the police car and give a speech to all of us on his bullhorn, calling for free speech at the university. Students surrounded that police car, with poor Jack Weinberg in it, for over twenty-four hours. We did everything we could, until finally the charges against Jack Weinberg were dropped. That was what set everything in motion.

On December 2, word got around that there was going to be a big sit-in at Sproul Hall, students and teachers alike. We all knew that if we participated, we'd be taken out by police. I was part of the crowd outside the building, but I couldn't decide whether to go into Sproul Hall. I didn't know if I could handle being dragged out and arrested. Friends were talking about it, and I was seeing people being dragged away. The message from the police was very plain: anybody who didn't get out immediately would be subject to arrest. And I debated, *Do I stay or go?* And that time I left. I felt guilty that I was scared, but I was.

### MARIO SAVIO'S SPEECH ON THE STEPS
### OF SPROUL HALL, DECEMBER 2, 1964

*There's a time when the operation of the machine becomes so odious, makes you so sick at heart that you can't take part! You can't even passively take part! And you've got to put your bodies upon the gears and upon the wheels, upon the levers, upon all the apparatus—and you've got to make it stop! And you've got to indicate to the people who run it, to the people who own it—that unless you're free the machine will be prevented from working at all!!*

*That doesn't mean—I know it will be interpreted to mean, unfortunately, by the bigots who run* The Examiner, *for example— That doesn't mean that you*

*have to break anything. One thousand people sitting down
some place, not letting anybody by, not [letting] anything
happen, can stop any machine, including this machine!
And it will stop!*

Everyone was instructed not to fight back with the police, so students were just taken out of Sproul Hall without a fight, very much in the way of Martin Luther King, Jr. The Free Speech Movement seemed so incredibly civilized to me. In fact, it *was* civilized with Mario Savio in charge: he was articulate, always wearing a tie and a coat, always respectful in his dissent. His speeches were so vivid and eloquent. They were about how we could live out there in the world all together. I just thought, *We can live differently, we can be peacefully united.* We could change the world. And I still feel that—even as unlikely as it looks these days. Mario Savio's oration had a kind of idealism that kept me afloat. We didn't just think we could stop the war—we thought we could create an entirely new sort of society.

Once the movement started, there were speakers out in Sproul Plaza every week, talking revolution. At lunchtime or after classes, everyone would pour into the plaza to hear someone speak over a bullhorn before the police showed up. In my simplistic and romantic thinking back then, I associated revolution with Che Guevara, and with Paris and the French Revolution. I thought of Che as a free spirit, fighting for what he believed in, and I knew the French Revolution was about the rich and the poor—the aristocracy who had this opulent life, and the people who were hungry in the streets of Paris rising up to change the status quo. The Free Speech Movement was its own sort of revolution, though a nonviolent one, thanks to Mario Savio. Nonviolence didn't make the message any less revolutionary—it made it even more potent for me, in a way. Shortly after the big sit-in, all the students went on strike. I didn't go to classes, and people were picketing in front of buildings—we were trying to shut down the university. I was so impressed that everyone was accomplishing what they were accomplishing—that's what happens when young people are in charge using the right words.

My mother knew all about the Free Speech Movement—I wrote her letters describing the events happening on campus, and she was totally in support of it. She was worried for my safety, certainly, but completely behind me, much as she was my whole life. (I didn't talk to my father about it much, but he wasn't as opposed to it as he might have been a decade before. My father had been a conservative throughout the 1950s, but I think being fired shook his whole worldview; he was very disillusioned. And over those next few years, working at the University of Michigan and later still at Berkeley, he inevitably became a liberal.) Not everyone, certainly, had supportive parents: one time Eleanor was on the phone with her mother and told her we were making breakfast for some friends who had just got out of jail, and her mother was horrified: "Harboring jailbirds?"

Mario Savio was a magnificent orator; everyone was mesmerized by what he was saying, and when we were listening to him, we felt like a powerful force on the campus and an example to everyone around the country. Much later, at Mario Savio's memorial service, I learned that he had majored in physics and poetry. And it was revelatory to me to find out he was Sicilian—he sat down with his family every night for dinner with a bottle of wine. I know that that was somehow part of his vision, a positive mind-set that we could change the world if we all came together in our communities—we could *do this*. His message encompassed the values of civil rights and pacifism, but the bigger message was about civilization, the beauty of a shared culture.

When the dominant culture behaves immorally, the way the United States was about the war, civil rights, and freedom of public expression, you begin to feel betrayed. That feeling started crystallizing for me while I was listening to Mario Savio. Somewhere along the way, in our country's rush to industrialization and consumerism, it began to feel like America had lost its humanity. There was a conservative oppression that I felt more and more as I got older. American culture in the 1950s and early '60s was simultaneously corrupt and puritanical, very closed-minded. I could tell it was about fear, for sure. But the people of the Free Speech

Movement were speaking my language; their message felt *right*. And the reason it all felt right, I think, was that my parents had taught me certain basic values: morality, empathy, frugality, love of nature, love of children. (I wish they'd passed along messages of openness about sex, too, but that was too much to expect from the 1950s.) Those were all values adopted by the counterculture—because, sadly, they had been forgotten by the culture at large.

When I finally declared my major, it ended up being French cultural history, from 1750 to 1850. The French Revolution—of course.

# CHAPTER 6

## *C'est si bon!*

For our unofficial, self-created junior year abroad, Sara Flanders and I flew to France. We had a flight from San Francisco to Luxembourg via New York and Iceland, on Icelandic Airlines, which was the cheapest possible way to get to Europe. (Icelandic Airlines's nickname was "The Hippie Airline," because it was the first real discount airline, and all the young people took it to get to Europe.) When our plane stopped over in New York, it picked up Louis Armstrong and his whole band—they were going to Reykjavik to play a concert. At that time, you could walk around during air travel, stand up, and smoke, and Louis Armstrong played on the plane—the whole band did! They all got off in Iceland, and when the plane took off again, it was pretty quiet.

Sara and I landed in Luxembourg—the end of the line. It was the middle of the night when we arrived, and we got straight onto a bus that would take us to Paris, five or six hours away. Basically from the border of France, there were almost no lights—you couldn't see anything out the windows.

*La Liberté Yankee éclairant le "Monde Libre"!*

POUR LE SOUTIEN A LA LUTTE DU PEUPLE VIETNAMIEN

# TOUS AU MEETING

Dans la cour de la Sorbonne
## JEUDI 1er AVRIL 1965 à midi

Cercle de Physique du SECTEUR SCIENCES de l'Union des Etudiants Communistes
3, Place Paul-Painlevé, PARIS-Vᵉ

I. C. P.

It was very eerie, almost like during a war when there's a blackout. Probably it was just about frugality and not wasting electricity. It was my first time outside the United States.

When we arrived in Paris, we stayed for a couple of nights at a tiny hotel in a fancy part of town, on a little back street across from the Chanel store and behind the Place Vendôme. My cousin Carolyn had told me about this hotel; she'd been in Paris before, and I have a feeling that her parents, my rich aunt Marian and uncle Harry, paid for us to have the hotel room for a couple of days. The room had heavy deep blue satin curtains, and you could close them so no noise or light could come through. Sara and I got to this hotel, went to bed, and then didn't wake up for a full twenty-four hours—we missed a whole day.

When we finally roused ourselves, we went down and ate in the hotel's restaurant—mostly because we were afraid to go out, afraid we might have to speak French to someone. The hotel dining room was everything you'd expect: high ceilings, crusty bread on the table, and white linens. Likely enough, Uncle Harry was paying for it all, but I was worried about how much it was going to cost, so we didn't order much. They served lunch in courses, and the first thing they brought out was *soupe de légumes*. I'd never tasted anything like it before. The soup had tiny cubed vegetables floating in a clear amber broth, delicate and simple and delicious. We savored it—I don't remember anything else we ate, only that sublime soup and a fresh baguette with butter.

Our trip to France had really been instigated by Sara, who had been wanting to go to Paris for a while. My mother had taught me to count from one to ten in French when I was little, during her friend Hope's stint in France, but that was more or less the extent of my knowledge; aside from that and the Latin I'd taken in fourth grade, I'd had no foreign language at all. But I'd liked the idea of doing a junior year abroad; Sara and I both thought it could be fun. The summer before we left, I worked as a receptionist at a bank to earn the money for our trip.

Our free hotel room didn't last long—we had to find another place to stay in the city, so we went around from hotel to hotel asking if they knew of any rooms to lease near our school on the Left Bank. Neither of us really spoke French; it was scary as hell. We finally found a temporary spot on the Rue des Écoles, in a fourth-floor walk-up, and later a room in an old house where you had to pay to take a bath at the communal bathroom. It was on Avenue des Gobelins in the fourteenth arrondissement, at the bottom of Rue Mouffetard. Looking back, we were incredibly lucky to be there, because Rue Mouffetard was a market street. Every day we walked up this winding cobblestone street lined with open stalls of fruits and vegetables on our way into the center of the Latin Quarter.

Sara and I were supposed to be going to the Cours de Civilisation Française at the Sorbonne. It wasn't part of UC Berkeley—we had just signed up on our own to take this

French civilization course. But I *never* went to class. I can't speak for Sara's attendance, but I went maybe only once or twice the whole year. Instead, we traveled all over, we hitchhiked, we went to art shows and music halls and little restaurants, we spent hours in marketplaces. We went to a lot of concerts; I heard the famous Soviet classical violinist David Oistrakh play at the Paris opera house. We were way up at the top of the balcony with free student tickets, as far from the stage as you could possibly be, but it didn't matter: he was playing the most beautiful Beethoven violin concerto. I had never heard anybody play like that—I was just carried away. I felt that same awe the first time I went into Chartres Cathedral and saw the stained glass there. And I fell in love with Sainte-Chapelle, on Île de la Cité, in the middle of Paris: the intimate size of it, and that breathtaking light through the stained glass when the sun comes in. You just felt like you were taken up by the beauty of the place. I loved that feeling: it was all around you, enveloping you. And the fact that people created this centuries ago! Sacred spaces like that are all designed to make you feel like you're being lifted up—that you should be part of that sacredness. I didn't know it then, but I was taking the *real* course in French civilization, even though I never made it to class.

Sara was the perfect travel companion, energetic and bright and culturally attuned. She always wanted to go to this or that museum to see such-and-such an artwork—like the sculptures at the Rodin Museum, or Manet's *Le Déjeuner*

*sur l'herbe* at the Jeu de Paume—and got me to do things I wouldn't have done otherwise. She was small, around my height, with light brown, very thick hair. She had lots of opinions. Back when we'd been in Alpha Phi at Santa Barbara, the other sorority sisters used to call Sara and Eleanor Plato and Aristotle, because they debated *everything* and were always embroiled in deep discussions. Sara was very confident and together, more sophisticated than I was: I was a bit scattered and unworldly. I wasn't leading things then. Sara read a lot of books and knew about trends in music—she was the first in our group of friends to recognize the Beatles, the Rolling Stones, Joan Baez, Bob Dylan. She had good taste in all things, and as we wandered around exploring France together, we were excited about the same places and foods and art.

We met boys, too. Ambroise was Sara's, and Jean-Didier Levy was mine. Ambroise and Jean-Didier were two French students who were going to the École Polytechnique—a very difficult school to get into—and they picked us up at some café or restaurant. It was Jean-Didier and Ambroise who really taught us to eat, and it had everything to do with choosing the right little restaurant every night for dinner. The four of us would go up and examine the menu posted out front and do a little critique: "Oh, they had *that* last night." "When do you think those oysters came in?" "Do we want a tarte Tatin?" "Have you tried their steamed mussels before?" We'd do that at *at least* three restaurants before choosing one. I was always impatient. Sara and I wanted to eat already, but we had to go evaluate them all first, while Jean-Didier and Ambroise argued and debated the relative merits of these places. They were probably showing off a little for us, but they always made good choices in the end, and we always sat down to great food. I'd never eaten like that before, and to eat with that kind of discernment made it so much more delicious.

We learned from Jean-Didier and Ambroise to have a green salad after the main dish, before the dessert; salad was meant to cleanse the palate and was dressed in a little delicious vinaigrette of olive oil and vinegar. I'd notice all the beautiful, unusual types of lettuce, particularly the little rosettes of mâche. (No rocket, though—that type of lettuce was still just a South of France thing.) Salad was never *not* part of the meal; we always had it before the dessert. Growing up we had wedges of iceberg lettuce in the winter with a bottle of Wishbone dressing. I liked the salty taste and the crunch, but I don't remember loving salad, really, until Paris. Salad was a big gift from the French; I adored it, and those green salads became a central part of my repertoire when I went back home.

Sara Flanders in our Paris apartment.

In the early 1970s, I went to the South of France and fell in love with mesclun, a mix of young salad greens that you really couldn't find anywhere outside a forty-five-minute radius of Nice. I loved it so much that I bought the seeds and planted them in my backyard so we could serve them at Chez Panisse. Mesclun became a staple on the menu, and we probably served salad grown in my backyard for a good five years, before farmers in Northern California realized the demand and began planting the seeds themselves. I think if there's one thing I'm responsible for in this country, something that I can take a little credit for, it's the propagation of real salad in the United States.

I was so proud of that mesclun salad that I took it to New York. In the late 1970s, after the restaurant had become established, Chez Panisse was one of Playboy magazine's twenty-five best restaurants in the country. (We were number seven!) The magazine invited each restaurant on the list to cook a dish at a big fête in New York City. Immediately I thought, I'm going to make a salad! That's my dish! My close friend Marion Cunningham, who had worked with the famous chef and food writer James Beard, said, "James could loan you a bowl, and you could make the dressing at his house!" (Marion, ironically enough, was a great lover of iceberg lettuce herself.) Sure enough, James Beard loaned me this beautiful wooden bowl, and I made our Chez Panisse version of the mesclun salad, with chervil and herbs and these beautiful little just-picked lettuces we brought on the plane from California.

All New York was invited, and every restaurant that had been on Playboy's list had a station. The other chefs, all men, were French and Italian, classically trained, representing restaurants from New

*York like Le Cirque. I respected everyone so much, and to be in that company was—well, I felt very honored. When I got there and looked around, I saw that all these chefs were making elaborate ice carvings, putting together their salmon quenelles. Someone down the way was preparing a lobster extravaganza. There was a picture of us that day before it started—I had on an antique maroon dress with little accordion sleeves, with very pale blue stones sewn around the neckline, surrounded by all these men in black suits. To stand there as the only woman, doing a green salad, I was so embarrassed. I almost died.*

*Amazingly, that salad was what people talked about the next day. I don't think I did anything with the presentation at all—I just served it on a plate! We didn't even have baked goat cheese with it, just, bang, lettuce. But that response really woke me up. It made me realize my naïveté, but I also felt a kind of pride in the simplicity of what we were doing at the restaurant. That I could think of going to New York and presenting green salad as our dish from Chez Panisse! I remember talking all night to anyone who came to my station about how James Beard had loaned me his salad bowl, as if to give me some credibility! Like, Well, at least he* thinks this salad is all right.

Dessert in Paris was tarte Tatin, the traditional upside-down apple tart—or you'd get a plate of *fraises des bois*. I'd never tasted anything like *fraises des bois* before, and initially I didn't even know what they were when they were brought to the table: a dish of little shriveled wild strawberries, and crème fraîche and a sugar shaker, and that was all. The taste was sublime: ethereal, sweet, complex, juicy.

We sampled a lot of cheeses during those meals—we'd always have cheese with our salad after the main course, and Jean-Didier and Ambroise would get to arguing again about the cheese: "Is this one ripe enough? Is that one the right temperature?" The whole nine yards. The one I really fell for was the Vacherin; it has a beautiful undulating top with a straw-orange crust, and it's ripe only in the fall and around Christmastime. It's semisoft, so when you cut into it, it begins to ooze, and it has almost a wild-mushroom taste. It's still one of my favorites.

*I'm always looking to learn more about great cheese. Much later I was very lucky to meet Jean d'Alos. Jean d'Alos was an* affineur *of cheese; he got that special designation,* affineur, *for his knowledge about raising and caring for cheeses. Our chef Jean-Pierre Moullé introduced me to him on a trip to Bordeaux—Jean-Pierre had grown up not far from Bordeaux and was very good friends with Jean d'Alos. It wasn't that I didn't know a lot about cheese at that point—I did, thanks to my trip to France, but I didn't know the true depth of it. Jean d'Alos goes to each farm that makes cheese when the cheeses are very young, and he raises them up until they're ready to serve. His actual cheese shop may have twenty-five cheeses, but then you descend into his cellar, and there are hundreds upon hundreds of wheels of cheeses, and he knows the exact moment to bring each one out. I'd never seen that before.*

*He told me two things I didn't know. One was that when you do a tasting of cheese, you always want to taste the inside first and then the rind, and then decide whether you want to eat them together. The rind is there to protect the cheese, and sometimes it's strong, sometimes it's not, sometimes it's complementary, and sometimes it's not. The second thing I learned was, you want to cut the cheese so that it echoes the original shape of the cheese form; if it's a tall, round cheese, you cut the slice very thinly, so you know it's tall and round. If you cut it poorly—if, for example, you cut the end off and give the softest part to some people and the hardest part to others—you don't really taste the cheese's full quality. And you always want to see the rind so you can marvel at it, or help identify the cheese because of it. It's all part of the beauty of cheese-making.*

*Jean d'Alos knew every one of the farmers and shepherds that he got the cheese from every year. We went with him into the Pyrenees to meet someone who made cheese, and that was revelatory, too. The shepherd called his sheepdogs to round up the sheep, and they all came running down the mountainside. Then he milked every one of them over the course of several hours, poured all the milk into a big pot on the fire, and formed the cheese with his hands in the warm milk. The work is unbelievable—he ended up with just one single cheese from all of that labor. I loved that you could watch the sheep eating the clover in the morning, then taste the clover in the milk when you drank it at night. The next morning we'd have the ricotta from that milk—the shepherd served it with rosehip jam that his grandmother made from the wild roses from the Pyrenean mountainside. It was one of the best breakfasts of my life.*

Sara and I would go out every morning and get a warm baguette—we could hardly wait to get it home to put the jam on it. I remember that first taste of apricot jam on a baguette that was still hot from the oven—I wanted to eat that every single day. And I did! Back then every corner in Paris had a place where baguettes were baked in a wood oven—in the mornings everyone went to the bakery, and you waited in line to get your baguette. We'd have more bread at lunch and even more with dinner; we always had some in the basket on the table. And they sold baguettes with butter and ham at the train station—we got those all the time when we traveled around France. Vendors would come up to the window of the train with baskets of little wrapped-up baguette sandwiches, and you could reach out the window and take one for your trip.

My first sense of wine didn't really come until France. There had been *no* wine in my parents' house when I was growing up; they drank only cocktails. When my father came home from work in the evenings, they had two scotch and waters each—or at least, my dad definitely had two. But there was no awareness of wine in our New Jersey "cuisine."

Sara and I knew we had to order wine with a meal in Paris, but we were afraid we'd make a mistake by ordering the *wrong* wine. So we never ordered red or white—we always ordered rosé. It seemed like the safe middle ground, and there were usually fewer rosé options on the menu. Maybe that's why I still love rosé to this day. People *were* drinking things like Coca-Cola in France at the time, so it wasn't that American products were absent—but the Coca-Cola was always poured into a glass with a lemon and a straw. And it wasn't a very big glass. But it cost a lot.

We were so intimidated by the Parisians—every time I opened my mouth, they would say, "*Je ne comprends pas, je ne comprends pas*"—I don't understand, I don't understand. I never wanted to speak, so we'd find people like Ambroise or Jean-Didier who would speak for us. (I *can* speak French now, but it's really English that I translate into French. I can communicate in French, but certainly not poetically and only after a bottle of wine.) I was most intimidated by the waiters. All the waiters were a little blasé and supercilious, even in small family restaurants. They didn't like Americans very much in Paris. Which was a shame, because I liked Paris *so* much. The feeling just wasn't mutual.

MARCH 30, 1965

*Hello Mother and Dad –*

*Right now I would be extremely happy-content-un-depressed since the weather has been perfect—just like ol' California—however as I told you, I lost my purse! . . .*

*As I was saying, the weather has been magnificent. Right now I'm sitting here in a blouse and skirt, window open, birds singing—slight breeze—the sun is about to set. And it was like this yesterday. I became over-enthusiastic and walked from our house to the Champs-Élysées! First*

*we went and sat in Luxembourg Gardens trying to tan our
anemic faces. The trees are just about ready to blossom—
you can see the green leaves coming out and the flowers look
splendid, flowerbeds filled with daffodils and trimmed with
violets—fountains everywhere you look. I think it's the
gardens that make Paris so unbelievably grand!! . . .*

*Friday night my French friend Jean-Didier took me
out to dinner and then showed me his slides of Africa and
Brazil, narrated in French. He speaks beautiful French and
knows about all kinds of things—unfortunately he knows
too much about the U.S. He constantly brings up the Ku
Klux Klan or some such thing to show how incompatible
the French culture is with the American. Depressingly
enough, he believes they are opposites. . . . I only wish I
could figure out all the good qualities of les États-Unis.
Any of my big ideas about democracy and liberty are
immediately challenged: "And what is the U.S. doing in
Vietnam? If you have any facts I'd like them. If it's a war
for liberation then why are we interfering?" Obviously
the French want us out. They'd like us out of commission.
What a mess! . . . Oh yes, this Latin-American friend of
Sara's said if he found an American girl's purse, he would
sell it—all—and give the money to the poor starving people
who don't have as much as the American capitalists! Here's
hoping a Brazilian didn't find my purse!*

*I could go on and on. I have millions of things to say but
my hand hurts and I have five more letters to write. Aunt*

*Ina wrote the nicest long letter—she's really wonderful.*
*Mother, tell her I'll be writing soon—Ellen also—God! I'm*
*going to be an aunt soon!—a fat one if I don't stop eating*
*these pastries and bread! Right now I couldn't be more*
*enthusiastic about everything if I tried. I love Paris! I love*
*traveling! I have a great desire to speak French again! I love*
*living! No, I suppose that's carrying it a bit far. I'm just so*
*happy I'm here. I wish you all were too. In fact I feel guilty*
*because you should have been here before me. I know I've*
*forgotten to say something important but then—*

> *Love,*
> *Alice*

My love of France was insatiable, so Sara and I would go
all over France on weekend trips on our Eurail Pass. We also
hitchhiked from Paris; we'd ride all the way to the end of the
métro in the right direction, then hitchhike from that place.
We'd get picked up by truck drivers—they seemed to usually
be older, very serious Frenchmen. We'd both sit in the cab up
in the front with him, and I'd sit there mute, while Sara made
conversation. But we had no fear and never had a bad time.
Hitchhiking just seemed so easy—I can't believe it now.

One of our trips was to Pont-Aven, a little town in Brit-
tany. Sara and I wanted to see the crucifix that inspired
Gauguin for his painting *Yellow Christ*. By the river near
Pont-Aven, out on the edge of town, almost in the coun-

try, we happened upon a little restaurant. We looked at the menu, went in, and got seats for lunch. It was on the second floor of a house, overlooking the landscape and the Aven River, and there were pink tablecloths on all the tables. The menu that day was cured ham and melon, whole trout with slivered almonds in browned butter, and a raspberry tart. No choices, just "This is what we're having today." Every dish was quietly sublime. That meal made a *very* big impression on both of us. I realized later that the food tasted so good because the trout probably came from the stream we could see out the window, the melons came from their garden, and the owners likely made their own *jambon*. It was one of those perfect little meals. Years later when I opened Chez Panisse, I looked back on that experience as a blueprint.

The dining room was filled with French gastronomes— or at least, they seemed that way to me, because they were so clearly enjoying the food. Everyone in the dining room was saying, *"Oh! C'est si bon!"* In other restaurants, the Frenchmen would normally just shrug and say, *"Eh, c'est bien."* They *never* said anything about any meal, even if it was fantastic— just *"C'est bien,"* in that blasé way. And here they were, exclaiming! Sara and I had never seen anything like it. It was the first time we'd seen the French be overtly enthusiastic about a meal. The men even asked the chef to come out so they could pay their compliments—to *her*. I just remembered: the chef was a woman.

. . .

When I think of Brittany, I go right to crêpes. It was one of those tastes I fell in love with: buckwheat crêpes, made on that little flat burner on street corners, thin as can be, spread with butter and a little sugar and splashed with Grand Marnier. There are crêpes, and then there are *crêpes*. The little white ones, the thin pancakes, that people roll and eat with jam can be very good. But this was a buckwheat crêpe that you could also eat with something savory if you wanted. In Brittany, you could have it stuffed with mussels. I did like the ones sold on the street corners in Paris, but when I went to Brittany, I really fell in love with buckwheat—and the hard apple cider! At that time in France there were special dishes from special places—crêpes were in Brittany, and a bit in Paris, but no place else. It was about local food. I was introduced to oysters in Brittany, too—that was the best place in the whole country to have them. Before our crêpes, we'd order a dozen oysters on the half shell. They were just out of the water, opened up in front of us, and bang, served. That's my idea of a perfect oyster: the Belon oyster.

Sara and I went to Versailles on one of our weekend trips. By that point, I was flirting with the idea of focusing my major on the French Revolution, because all the courses I'd been drawn to—music, art, history—fit into that period in Europe, from 1750 and 1850. Versailles was what the whole revolution was about. It's hard not to be astonished by the opulence and extravagance of the place; anyone who goes there can understand why the people revolted, seeing all that excess. And for me, coming straight from the radicalism of Berkeley and the Free Speech Movement, it was even more obvious. But fascinating, too. Extraordinary things happened there in the seventeenth and eighteenth centuries with art and architecture—and, I learned later, with the garden.

*Much, much later I went back to Versailles with a garden scholar, Antoine Jacobsohn, who was teaching me about what they were doing there. Versailles was where French intensive gardening started, because the king wanted fruits and vegetables that were available*

*sooner and were better than anybody else's. He wanted to get a jump on the season. French intensive gardening means making the most out of a small plot of land, getting it to produce the most food possible; it means using animal manure in the soil to fertilize plants, or growing plants next to a warm wall so they will yield fruits sooner. I didn't know that Versailles was where it all started until I saw this incredible garden—they managed to feed ten thousand people from it with the gardening methods they invented. And I always wonder how I can feed ten thousand people out of a garden.*

*Another thing I learned was that, in the eighteenth century when they were feeding lots of people in the châteaux, the cooks used to have ripening rooms. Individual fruits were placed on special racks, designed so the different types of fruits wouldn't touch each other as they ripened. I know this is rarefied, the existence of an entire room dedicated to ripening fruit, but the concept was right; fruits shouldn't be touching each other when they're ripening. This knowledge about varietals and how to care for them was happening all over France, not just at Versailles. I recently saw one of the most mind-blowing books about figs in a library on agriculture in France. Every fig had a hand-painted illustration, with the name of the fig below it and a full description of its taste and what it looked like. There were probably ten figs to a page, and this book was two inches thick! I thought,* I don't know anything about figs! *At this point in my life, I might know fifteen varietals, tops, and I could maybe describe the way they taste and how they look. But to know that that kind of biodiversity existed, and to witness that type of detail and this culture's deep interest in it, just took my breath away.*

For Easter vacation, Sara and I took the train to Spain—not thinking about the fact that it was still Franco's Spain at that time. I stood up that whole train ride down to Madrid, for ten hours—it was packed because it was spring break. And, of course, *nothing* was open in Madrid when we got there—no museums, no restaurants, nothing—because it was Easter. There were lots of Easter processions going on, but that was it. So we thought, well, we'll go to Barcelona, maybe we can find something better there, and Sara talked about wanting paella. I don't know how we got out to Barcelona, but we did and stayed in a dismal little room. I saw people down on their knees in the streets, crawling up to the church for some sort of masochistic Easter ritual—carrying a cross, flagellating themselves. We did eat seafood paella there, but it seemed so oily. At a tapas bar, I met a blond expat who tried to seduce me by feeding me whole shrimp with their shells on, and I *was* seduced; I went home with him. Then I got hideously sick from eating those shrimp—it felt like a nightmare. Sara and I couldn't wait to return to France. It was such a tremendous relief to get back to what we knew in Paris.

At the end of our year, Sara may have taken the exam at the Sorbonne, but I don't think I did. I certainly didn't pass. Before we went back to Berkeley, we used our Eurail Pass to take a "grand tour" of Europe on what little money we had left: Copenhagen, Venice, Rome, stopping in all the big cities, but for only about two minutes each. It was so horribly hot that I went swimming in the Trevi Fountain, though, of course, you weren't supposed to.

Sara and I took a train to Rotterdam to take the student ship home to New York. The *Groote Beer* was run by a discount travel organization that had cheap fares for students. On the dock waiting for the ship, I met another student from Berkeley who was traveling abroad, Tim Savinar, who had just come from Greece. I instantly fell in love with Tim: he was very tan and slim, funny and sensitive and talkative, and was such an intellectual.

I read Thomas Mann's *The Magic Mountain* on that ship because Tim had recommended it to me. It was about tuberculosis patients isolated in a sanitarium on top of the highest mountain in Switzerland; the everyday isolation and loneliness of it pushes you into an introspective place. I dove into that book, immersed myself in it. After a while, our ship across the Atlantic felt like a floating sanitarium—and considering how seasick I got, it practically was. It was a good five or more days to get back to New York on the *Groote Beer*; my cabin with Sara was below sea level, and the food got worse and worse the whole trip, until pretty soon we were having only cabbage and tripe. At one point I had had enough; I went to the front of the ship with Tim and stood on the bow for hours. I simply could *not* go back inside to face that again—it was too much, with the unrelenting smell of tripe and cabbage penetrating everything.

I was crazy about Tim. He was the first man I'd met whom I thought I could bring home to my family. He was so friendly and open and kind. He was a student at Cal too, so we dated for a little while back in Berkeley, but finally he had to sit me down and tell me he wasn't in love with me. I don't remember how long we dated; not long enough. (In the end, he married my good friend Patty Unterman, so we've become lifelong friends. Tim was even the head of the board of directors of Chez Panisse for many years.)

Tim was also a distraction from what I was really feeling: I was profoundly sad to be leaving France. I didn't quite know what I was going back to in Berkeley—I knew I had to finish school, but I didn't feel excited about it. I felt like I had changed in some way, that I'd tapped into a way of life in France that had shifted things for me irrevocably, though it wasn't clear what that change was exactly.

Tim Savinar
waiting on the dock.

A bit later Jean-Didier asked me to marry him. He sent me an airplane ticket to come back to France. I liked him, but I definitely wasn't thinking about him like that. I was in love with France, not with Jean-Didier.

*Many years later, I got a letter in the mail saying I was being awarded France's Légion d'honneur. It's one of the most meaningful awards I've ever received. I learned so much from the French. And I realized when I got that award that I hadn't just taken French cooking home with me, I brought the Slow Food culture of France home. That's why I got the Legion of Honor, I think—because I was preserving and expressing something of the culture that the French thought was valuable. That doesn't mean there weren't times in the late 1970s and early '80s when French patrons would come to Chez Panisse and say, "That's not cooking, that's shopping." But my whole library of French cookbooks that go back to the beginning of gastronomy in France were the foundation of Chez Panisse. Brillat-Savarin wrote some of the most important ideas: "The destiny of nations depends upon the manner in which they were fed." And "We are what we eat." Those are the sorts of ideas that I'm still trying to get out there in the world.*

*I had been recommended for the award by the French Consulate General in San Francisco, so I received it there. During the ceremony, when they were putting the pin on me, the medal fell to the ground—and broke!*

*"Oh my God!" I said.*

The man pinning it just leaned over and picked it up. "Well, they're made in China now. You can just get another one when you're in Paris."

I couldn't believe it—they broke so easily because the Légion d'honneur medal isn't made in France anymore! The medal itself is no longer valuable in the way it once was.

The next time I was in Paris, I went to get it fixed. "I'd love to wear the medal on a ribbon around my neck," I told the man repairing it.

The man looked at me in horror and said, "You don't *wear it on a ribbon. You wear it on a pin. On your left side.*" He was really adamant that I not put it anywhere else other than where it was meant to be: *above my heart.*

Me in the front row of a women's peace march
in San Francisco, circa 1966.

# CHAPTER 7

# Politics Is Personal

When I got back from France, Eleanor and Sara and Betsy and I moved into an old Victorian house on Dwight Way. I felt like *the* most sophisticated person. I just thought I knew everything. I wanted to live like the French. As luck would have it, a Frenchman, Pierre Furlan, lived downstairs from us in the basement apartment, and he would pop into our lives every so often. A French journalist friend of Pierre's, Jean Contenay, gave us Owsley Stanley's LSD one time, as a housewarming present; Owsley's LSD was the first and the best, back when it was still legal—his stuff was what Ken Kesey, the Beatles, and Timothy Leary all took. Jean stayed in our attic for a few nights after he interviewed Henry Miller in Big Sur, and gave us three tabs of LSD as a parting gift—picked up from Big Sur, probably. LSD blew my mind—literally. It was an out-of-body experience for me. I really thought I was up on the ceiling looking down at Eleanor, and I suspected I might never come back down again. Everything was buzzing and moving, and I had to be very careful what I thought about. If I thought about bugs in the grass, I could suddenly see them everywhere; if I thought about the grain of the wood in the floorboards, I could see the molecules moving. That was it for me—I never took LSD again.

Sometimes when Eleanor and Sara and Betsy and I were experimenting with French recipes, Pierre Furlan would call upstairs, ask what we were having for dinner, and come up and cook with us. He knew how to cook and would make corrections and additions or give bits of advice if we were going off the rails. At the time, I was making a lot of buckwheat crêpes and watching plenty of Julia Child. She was speaking my language. She was very funny and grounded—she'd drop the chicken on the floor, pick it up, and keep right on going—and I wanted to master the art of French cooking, exactly that. I did buy her book, *Mastering the Art of French Cooking*, but it was more or less incomprehensible to me; it had no pictures, long and detailed recipes, and lots of writing about precision. It was daunting. But luckily there was the TV show—I loved her manner, and she was a Francophile just like I was.

*I've always said that Julia Child's show allowed Chez Panisse to flourish. And that's the truth—if Julia hadn't prepared people for French cooking, our little French restaurant never would have worked. I got to know her years later, and after the restaurant had been open for a decade or so, I filmed an episode with Julia for one of her shows. We were a funny pair: Julia was over six feet tall and I am five foot two, so she towered over me. I was clearly not preparing food the way a chef was supposed to—and she knew it. I was pitting olives with my fingers, and she'd say, in that fluting voice of hers, "Oh! Is that how you pit an olive, Alice? How fascinating!" I'm much more about using my hands when I'm cooking. On another Julia Child show, I was tasked with making a salad. I was tossing it with my hands, tasting a leaf every so often—I think when you dress a salad with your hands, it's easier to tell when you have the right amount of oil and vinegar on the leaves. Julia looked down at me doing this, my hands covered in vinaigrette, and said, "Well, it is possible to do this with two spoons, isn't it, Alice?" And I said, "Oh, of course. I would normally do it with two spoons!" But secretly, I wouldn't.*

In 1966 I started working for Bob Scheer's campaign for Congress. Bob would become terribly important in my life. He was a radical journalist for *Ramparts* and had written a white paper for the Center for the Study of Democratic Institutions in Santa Barbara called *How the United States Got Involved in Vietnam*. I read that paper, a brilliant exposé that outlined the shocking facts about how we had become embroiled there. He opened our eyes to the tragedy of what was happening in Vietnam. The paper became a manifesto for the antiwar movement, being passed around from person to person on campus—a natural extension of the Free Speech Movement.

Jerry Rubin at a Vietnam Day Committee
demonstration shortly before we met.

I'm always drawn to great orators. I'm in awe of those
who can speak in a way that's universal, taking complex
things and communicating them simply and with clarity,
where everybody gets it. And Bob Scheer was one of the
best. He was running for Congress as one of the first anti–
Vietnam War candidates, and he came to UC Berkeley to
give a speech shortly after the paper was written. I felt like
he was one of the few people out there in politics who was
actually telling the truth. I imagine that's how my mother
must have felt listening to Adlai Stevenson. When I heard
Bob Scheer speak, that was it: I wanted to work for him. He
galvanized people with his words. I told him as much after

his talk, and he said, "Well, come on board. You can drive me from place to place."

I met Jerry Rubin around that time because of the Scheer campaign—he was an infatuation of mine. Jerry was an antiwar activist hanging around UC Berkeley who wasn't supposed to be on campus. He had a more aggressive, agitprop attitude than Bob—Jerry felt like an anarchist at times—and he later started the Youth International Party, the Yippies, with Abbie Hoffman. I saw a lot of Jerry and was strangely attracted to him, and we walked around town together a lot. I don't remember what we talked about for those few months, as I followed him around, but I felt like I was in a secret society, going into rooms with all these radicals and revolutionaries. He looked like a character out of a noir film, wearing a long brown overcoat and a 1940s felt fedora with the brim pulled low. We didn't date, but I suppose I was a secret admirer of his. I think he was more interested in politics than in sex.

Around then Richie Thomas, my middle school secret admirer, was on his way to Vietnam. He didn't want to go but had been asked to be a translator, so he came out West to learn Mandarin Chinese at the language school in Monterey. During his time off, he would come up to Berkeley to see me. We saw each other a few times and fell in love for a moment. Richie was really, really smart and a great writer; he had a motorcycle that we'd take across the bridge to San

Francisco to get Irish coffee at Buena Vista Café down by the waterfront. Richie had money, or at least a little more than I did, and would stay at our house on Dwight and buy me Cointreau so I could use it in my crêpes. Eventually his school told him that he wasn't allowed to come up to Berkeley anymore. I didn't make it easy on him. I was into heavy antiwar indoctrination at that time, working for Bob Scheer, and it made Richie uncomfortable, since he knew he had to go to Vietnam. I was so sad for him. He kept trying to tell me that he'd be in a special place, that he was just going to be a translator, that I shouldn't worry about him.

So he went to Vietnam—and I stopped hearing from him. I suspected it was such an extreme experience that he couldn't even talk to me. I tried to contact him many times— later on, I reached his mother, who said he'd gone back to his hometown and had married his high school sweetheart. I thought I understood it many years later, after watching the film *Apocalypse Now*. It was what happened to so many people who experience something so horrifying: they need to separate from the confusing parts of their past. Or, who knows—maybe he just found it hard to talk to *me*.

Sometime that year Eleanor, Sara, and I all marched to Berkeley's Herrick Hospital; Sara had announced, "We need to go down there and get the Pill." I was a little embarrassed and probably wouldn't have gone if Sara and Eleanor hadn't been with me. We went to the clinic, had our exams, got our prescriptions, and that was that. In some ways, the 1950s and early '60s were a horrible time to be a woman. I knew girls who were forced to go to Mexico for risky backroom abortions. At Santa Barbara, all the women got married immediately after their senior year, so there was no room for them to be anything but a wife and mother—and certainly none of them would admit to having sex before marriage. I had presumed that would be my life. But in Berkeley, it was acceptable by the mid-1960s to move in with your boyfriend instead of getting married—that was a big change.

Even so, a lot was still left unsaid; Sara got *so* mad at us after she proposed getting the Pill, because until she'd brought up the subject, she hadn't known the rest of us were already having sex. We were all such close friends, living in the same house, and somehow none of us had thought to talk about it.

"There's *nothing* attractive about being a twenty-one-year-old virgin," she lamented.

It was a huge, strange, transitional moment; not five years earlier I had been terrified I might be pregnant, terrified I had ruined my life, barely understanding how the whole process worked. In that way, the Pill changed my life. You didn't worry about pregnancy ever again—you worried about other things, but not about that. After the Pill, I felt less guilty about having sex; you could meet somebody you liked, and one way to find out whether you wanted to get to know him better was to sleep with him. We joked that it was just like that Rodgers and Hammerstein song "Getting to Know You." Suddenly we were all free and easy. After the Pill, this was completely normal—the Pill liberated us, it equalized men and women, and it kept us safe. It was not my mother's world anymore. Of course, we found out ten years later about the high doses of estrogen in the Pill, and all the side effects and dangers that came along with that first version of it. But we didn't know any of that at the time.

Various opportunities were popping up in Berkeley to explore "alternative" ways to find dates. Sara and I decided to participate in an embryonic version of computer dating—perhaps we were emboldened by being on the Pill, but more than likely we were just curious to try something new. This was considered *extremely* modern. (I can't tell you how basic it was compared with the way things are done today.) Sara and I each filled out long questionnaires, almost like SAT test forms, and our answers were punched into a stack of computer cards. These cards were then fed into some machine and the results were spit out with our "perfect mates" written on them. Oddly, Sara and I both ended up with two very similar men: highly intellectual psychologist/sex therapist types. I don't know what we had each answered on our forms to attract men like these. It was probably, as Sara said later, because she and I were the same height—that all-important variable! Regardless, our computer-generated dates didn't come to much—at least not for the sex therapist and me.

I found my way to David Goines's print shop in June 1966. We were having Bob Scheer's leaflets printed there—I was the "press liaison," and I came by every afternoon at four p.m. to pick them up. I took in the amazing big printing press machines and the beautiful ink and the pungent smell of the press running. David was there in the middle of it all, designing and making incredible posters and teaching calligraphy. He wore the same uniform to the print shop every day, jeans and a blue work shirt and a vest and brown boots. He had curly hair and little wire-rimmed spectacles,

like a cross between Trotsky's and John Lennon's. He always carried a pocket watch and had a Mont Blanc fountain pen tucked into his vest that he would hand-fill with ink. It almost felt like he had dropped in from another century—his considered speech, his manners, everything.

David was a perfectionist in all things, even food, and made his espresso just *so*: he always got the perfect beans and ground them with a hand grinder. He started writing me little calligraphed notes with beautiful drawings. One day he invited me to his house for cognac and espresso—he lived in an old Victorian with a turret, around the corner from the print shop—and after that, I sort of never left. That's when we first started dating.

You are cordially invited for coffee & cognac at 5 p.m. this afternoon at my house. Davidov

Meeting David opened my mind to print and showed me a new way of looking at the world. I'd walk through Berkeley noticing typefaces everywhere. How books are printed, how signs are made, and how letters are etched makes what is being read that much more valuable. Things that read well and are well designed have a different feeling. It's like going into the Lincoln Memorial and seeing those letters carved in stone—you go away awestruck.

*Letterpress printing and graphic design have been woven through Chez Panisse in a big, big way. It's a visual cue, a way of preparing the room to bring people fully into the experience. When something is well printed and well designed, even a menu, people take it more seriously. It has a presence and reflects on what they're about to eat. Printing and design are underrated, from the tiniest business card to a fifteen-foot-high billboard (though I don't believe in billboard advertisements, truly—I think they should be banned). The way you communicate is almost as important as what you're communicating. It's what Marshall McLuhan said: the medium is the message. The classic ways that people have communicated have civilization in them. Tradition is built in. But when we communicate now, we don't think about details like typeface and white space. You can lose people's attention just by not leaving enough white space around words. That's why I'm so obsessed with the design of the books we've published at Chez Panisse. The cookbooks come from a place of trying to inform rather than to indoctrinate—*

*not shouting at people, the way advertisements do, but invit-*
*ing them in, seducing them with illustrations. You don't want to*
*overdesign—you want to maintain clarity and simplicity. It's*
*hard for me to read something that's cluttered, with loud colors. It*
*gets too confusing.*

I loved going to the press to watch David, or his fellow
printer and friend Tom Weller, mix colors for posters. It was
a dream, like watching someone cook for you in the kitchen.
Printing is such an art—it's got magic in it. I loved the possibility of printing news and reaching people in an effective
and artful way, projecting your message out there.

David was and is an incredible artist. For one of my birth-
days, he designed a bookplate especially for me, hand carved
with my initials, ALW, with a tree and a little bird up above.
*Sic transit gloria mundi* was one of David's favorite mottoes.
It's a common Latin phrase: "Thus passes away the glory of
the world." Sometimes, when the spirit moved him, he would
meticulously hand-draw that motto into my cookbooks on
a little banner above my bookplate stamp. I think he must
have thought it funny—it sounds a bit dark, but it made perfect sense at the time. And in a way, it was a call to grab onto
the glory and beauty of the world while it is there in front of
you. David was a romantic—and I really love romantics.

David had been involved in the Free Speech Movement
from the very beginning; he was the first student to be
thrown off campus and expelled. He had set up one of those

tables in Sproul Plaza and was trying to pass out leaflets about political activities, and that was what led to his expulsion. In August 1967 he was sent to the Santa Rita jail for a thirty-day sentence as a result of his political activism. That was scary for me, and though I considered myself an activist, I felt I didn't have the strength to risk going to jail. We could go see him on visiting days, and we drove out there whenever we could. The jail was an hour's drive over the hills from Berkeley in the valley past Pleasanton. It wasn't an imposing place, certainly fenced and all of that, but it didn't look impressive. We were searched when we got there, and there were always bars between us—I wasn't allowed to bring any food, though I would have liked to. David was so courageous, constantly reassuring me, always saying, "Don't worry about me. Everything's all right, we're okay here." I visited every Sunday with his mother. He wrote beautifully calligraphed letters to me from the jail. Later he wrote a long book called *The Free Speech Movement*. When he finally got out, we drove out to Santa Rita and picked him up.

David's phone number is one of the few I still know by heart.

In 1967 my older sister Ellen, her husband, Bob Pisor, and their two year-old son, David, my little nephew, were all on their way to Vietnam; they came through Los Angeles, and I went down to visit them at my parents' house. Bob was a journalist for the *Detroit News* and was being sent to Vietnam to report, so the whole young family was going to be stationed in Saigon for a while. Ellen had married Bob as soon as she graduated from college, as I had assumed would happen to me. Bob had a great voice—both for singing and for reporting. I thought their marriage was a great thing; Ellen and Bob were in love from the first time they met, stayed in love all through college, and are still madly in love now. They went to Wooster College in Ohio, and their wedding was in Columbus—Bob's family was from there. I was Ellen's bridesmaid; I was a sophomore in high school, and our family was still living in Michigan then. The trumpet player on the altar played Vivaldi's Trumpet Voluntary as we processed down the aisle—this triumphant, joyful music. (Apparently shortly after Ellen was married, my mother sat her down and explained that she needed to learn about birth control— something that my mother had never known about when she was a newlywed—and urged her to seriously consider not having more than two children. Ellen ultimately followed her advice—two children, no more—long before she became a proponent of zero population growth!)

On that trip to Los Angeles, we were all hanging out together, and Ellen was making a beef Stroganoff with cream sauce and canned mushrooms. I berated her for not using fresh mushrooms. Ellen explained that there were no fresh mushrooms in the Midwest in winter, but I made her go to the market with me to buy fresh ones. And it was an entirely different—and better—dish; Ellen admitted it.

**BOB SCHEER** was a Fellow and Teaching Assistant in Economics at the University of California.

Bob is Foreign Affairs Editor of **Ramparts** magazine and director of its explosive study of Oakland. He has traveled extensively in Southeast Asia, twice in the past year. He is the author of **Cuba, Tragedy in Our Hemisphere** and **How the United States Got Involved in Vietnam.**

Bob and his wife, Anne, have been active in peace and civil rights demonstrations in the Bay Area.

Bob and Anne Scheer

**Register Democratic by April 14 • Vote Tuesday, June 7**

# Bob SCHEER
## PEACE • JOBS • FREEDOM

If you want to work or contribute to the campaign or find out more about it, or be registered to vote — call one of the offices below:

### SCHEER for CONGRESS headquarters:

| 2214 Grove St. | 2495 Telegraph Ave. | 4529 Grove St. |
| Berkeley | Berkeley | Oakland |
| 549-0690 | 848-0655 | 658-9570 |

I loved little two-year-old David, and I had a very sweet time with him in L.A. But it was really terrifying for me—I was with this adorable, wonderful kid, hugging and kissing in the backyard, and knowing so much about Vietnam and the horrors over there. But Ellen and Bob were determined to go and ended up living in Saigon for a year, even during the Tet Offensive. And oh God, yes, I was worried—we were all so fearful of what might happen.

Technically I was still in school, but I was consumed by Vietnam and Bob Scheer's campaign for Congress. As Bob's assistant, I drove him to the houses or meeting halls where he spoke; I'd stand at the back of the room and listen to him.

I'm pretty sure all this was volunteer work—no pay involved. At a house in North Berkeley, an old Arts and Crafts home up in the hills, people crowded in to hear him speak about the Vietnam War—he could always electrify a room. Eleanor remembers that I was really running the campaign out of our apartment—Bob Scheer would be in our living room next to the phone, and I'd be working three rooms away; the phone would ring right next to him, and Bob would call out, "Alice! Answer the phone!" Eleanor was very annoyed by that, but it didn't bother me.

How amazing is it when you're in sync with someone, and they're saying everything you want to say but better! Bob Scheer was so brilliant, so articulate—I totally believed him. I knocked on every door in West Oakland with complete guts, giving out "Scheer for Congress" leaflets and buttons. West Oakland had turned into a very poor area after World War II, inhabited by the African American community who had come up from the South to work in the shipyards. I was sure everyone would understand why Bob Scheer should win—I had total confidence in him. And the outcome was very, very close. He won over 45 percent of the vote and even carried Berkeley. But he lost the election. I was profoundly depressed. I still am. I remember abandoning all my faith in the democratic process after that—I didn't believe change could happen anymore. I mean, I really lost hope.

# CHAPTER 8

## Summers of Love

One afternoon in June 1967, I walked out of David's house, and every house on the block was playing the Beatles' *Sgt. Pepper's Lonely Hearts Club Band* album. Every house. It was warm outside, and you could stand in the street and listen to the music coming from the open windows. *That* was what the summer of 1967 was like in Berkeley. Things were dark at that time in the country, but the Beatles brought back hope—their music was a message from England that was joyful and honest and deeply inclusive. Everybody related to that music. It was bigger than a person being elected into office—it was about love. And it brought me back. That was my Summer of Love.

I was officially living with David by then, in the Victorian house with the turret. We had a big old table, and we always had lots of people over for dinners—food, like music, was a grounding force, a way to return to what felt good and right and hopeful about the world, bringing us all together around a table where we could talk politics or play cards. I was making crème caramel and chocolate mousse *all* the time those days, because *everybody* liked those two things. I was making other dishes, too, but the home runs were the chocolate mousse and the crème caramel. I'd add cognac or Grand Marnier in place of a recipe's vanilla extract—that was my big culinary secret. I served that mousse one time, and David said, "I hope you know this has more protein in it than the average Vietnamese peasant has in a week." To David, everything was political; to me, too, but I wasn't about to give up the chocolate mousse.

When I started preparing all those dinners, I can't say I had any consciousness of being a cook yet. I was interested in eating. When I got back from France, I wanted to eat like the French, and the only way I could get those flavors again was to make the dishes myself. No restaurants in Berkeley and San Francisco were cooking that way—or if they were, I couldn't afford them. The process of cooking was demanding—I had a certain taste in my mind, and I *really* wanted to get the food there. And I couldn't do it at first. I could never please myself except when I went to chocolate mousse or crème caramel, and people liked those no matter what.

David and I came up with an idea to do a newspaper column about cooking for the *San Francisco Express Times*, a paper that was around for only about nine months; I wanted to turn all the people who worked on the *Express Times* on to real food. It all went back to France—I had been awakened to taste there, and I wanted everybody to be awakened the way I had been. I was convinced I could win people over if I fed them the right food, if I got them to taste something that they'd never had before.

That's how the column "Alice's Restaurant" was born. David agreed to calligraph it and do a block print for each recipe, and I'd gather ideas for the recipes from my friends who cooked. I'd taste something a friend had made, write down the recipe, and ask if I could use it for the column. I'd make the recipe myself, see if people liked it, and if they did, I'd include it. I don't know that I fully gave credit where credit was due on those recipes—it's hard with a recipe, though, because each one *is* so fluid, and if you change a couple things in it, it almost becomes your own. But it's important to recognize the people and the history and the traditions behind recipes, to know what they're building upon. (That's why I consider all the Chez Panisse cookbooks to be collaborations, with inspirations from a lot of different cooks. And once those recipes of ours are out there in the world, I think, they belong to everybody—the more, the merrier.)

My sense of taste had been awakened in France, but it wasn't limited to the French cuisine. We published recipes for everything from the simplest Moroccan carrot salad to a beef borscht from somebody's Russian grandmother. I was obsessive about making every dish that went into that column, and about plenty of other dishes, too. For *boeuf bourguignon*, I'd make a real beef stock with beef shank; or a *salade crudités* with carrots and leeks and a vinaigrette; or eggs mayonnaise, a very classic French dish that consists of hard-cooked eggs with a loose handmade mayonnaise drizzled liberally on top. I had to make mayonnaise many times before I got the emulsion right and finally succeeded by sticking half a raw potato on the end of a fork and whisking the mayonnaise with it—somebody's grandmother had told me about that trick. Amazingly, it worked. And so I wrote that exact instruction into my mayonnaise recipe for the column: "Beat together two egg yolks in a wide bottom bowl using a fork stuck into a half potatoe [sic] with the flat side exposed." Because it worked for me. That's truly how I made mayonnaise every time, at least until I got to Chez Panisse. Crazy.

Once I got a recipe right, David would calligraph it and illustrate it straightaway, no editing, and then send it in. I couldn't control what he decided to draw—I just let him do whatever he wanted. For one recipe he chose to draw a castle and a medieval soldier on a horse, and, of course, the dish, marinated tomatoes, had nothing at all to do with castles and knights! But when somebody's such an incredible artist, as David is, there's not much you can say. Plus, he was doing it all for free—for love. Most important, the illustrations were always beautiful, and people collected and adored them. A few years later David compiled all the "Alice's Restaurant" columns into a portfolio called *Thirty Recipes Suitable for Framing*, which sold well enough to get him the money to buy his own printing studio.

David later made posters for Chez Panisse's birthday every year—sometimes you couldn't *imagine* what he had been thinking, because the image had seemingly nothing to do with Chez Panisse. And then, sometimes, it *really* did. Who knew what had been going on in his brilliant head? But the art that resulted was always unique and distinctive. His work became emblematic of Berkeley, and you saw it all over.

After I came back from France, I realized that maybe I was tasting things differently from other people. There was a cookware store and bookshop in Berkeley called the Kitchen that I loved to visit; it was run by Gene Opton, a woman with strawberry-blond hair and braids who wore these odd

LA SAUCE MAYONNAISE

it is essential to begin with all the ingredients at room temperature · beat together two egg yolks in a wide bottom bowl using a fork stuck into half a potatoe with the flat side exposed · beat in ½ teaspoon dijon mustard · ½ teaspoon of salt · & ½ teaspoon wine vinegar · & ½ teaspoon of confectioner's sugar · when the mixture is smooth · begin pouring a constant thread of olive oil · the better the quality of the oil, the better the taste · stir vigourously as the oil is added · when about ½ cup of oil has been poured · the mixture should begin to emulsify · continue · adding a sprinkling of vinegar every so often · after several additions of vinegar · switch to lemon juice · it is possible to use as much as 2½ cups of oil · adding lemon when necessary to insure the consistency & taste ·

little peasant blouses and dirndl smocks, like something out of *Heidi*. Gene gave me the English food writer Elizabeth David's cookbook, and it was a ray of sunshine. She was another Francophile who had been transformed after a visit to France; I identified with her walking through the French markets, discovering the flavors of steamed mussels, reveling in the mâche salad.

RUSSIAN BEEF BORSCH

Begin the borsch well in advance of serving · either in the morning · or the night before · In a deep eight quart kettle · place a large beef-marrow bone · four pounds of beef shin · one tablespoon of salt · & two quarts plus one cup of water · Cover & bring to a boil · then skim the surface · Reduce heat & simmer · covered · for one hour.

Next · add four medium tomatoes · quartered · one · quartered onion or chopped leek · one stalk of chopped celery · three sprigs of parsley · six whole black peppercorns & a bay leaf · Simmer two hours longer and remove from heat · Lift out the beef & set it aside · Remove & discard the marrow bones · Strain the soup & skim off the fat · this should leave about nine cups of liquid · Return soup & beef to the kettle & add 2½ cups of shredded beets · three cups of coarsely shredded red cabbage · 1½ cups of thickly sliced carrots · one cup of chopped onion · two table-spoons of freshly snipped dill · ¼ cup of cider vinegar · two tablespoons of sugar · one teaspoon salt & one large package of "whites" dried boletus mushrooms · Bring to a boil · reduce heat & simmer covered for thirty minutes - or until vegetables are tender · Remove from heat & refrigerate for six to eight hours · Before serving heat gently to boiling & then turn into a large tureen · Top each serving with sour cream & serve with piroshki ·

It was so lucky that I learned to cook from her—she was able to write about food in this great free-form, elegant prose. Her recipes are in paragraph form, without specific measurements: "Put in a handful of this," or "Add a pinch of salt." Or she would say something like "Get a beautiful butter lettuce and dress it lightly"—that would be her whole recipe. Which meant you had to actually *think* about the cooking: *Is this what she wants me to do? Maybe she wanted me to do it this other way?* You were provoked to think about it and rely on your own senses. I'd have little conversations with Elizabeth David every day while reading her book.

*Something can be lost in writing down a recipe. People can become so focused on measuring ingredients that they're not tasting as they go along, and at the end of it, they don't have the confidence to cook without a recipe. I like great cookbook writers like Elizabeth David, Richard Olney, Diana Kennedy, and Madhur Jaffrey, who describe the raw materials in a beautiful way, then encourage you to go out to the farmers' market and experience it all for yourself. That's where the real learning happens. The famous French chef Alain Ducasse says 85 percent of cooking is shopping; it may even be more than that, it might be 90 percent. But that's not, of course, going to the supermarket—it's going to the farmers' market, or out into your backyard, finding what's ripe and beautiful and alive and in season. This is my favorite recipe: "Go get some perfectly ripe figs in August, put them on a plate, and eat them."*

*No, my favorite recipe is: "Go cut some mint from the garden, boil water, and pour it over the mint. Wait. And then drink." That's my favorite recipe.*

I spent hours and hours poring over *Larousse Gastronomique*, which my parents gave me for Christmas 1966. *Larousse Gastronomique* is an alphabetical reference tool, a formidable encyclopedia of French food, and I'd lose myself in the diagrams of all the types of classic copper pots: sauté pan, frying pan, *petit* casserole, oval casserole for chicken *en cocotte*, stew pan, large stockpot, pan for steaming potatoes, braising pan, two-sided copper pan for making *pommes Anna*. Every pan had a specific shape and a specific purpose, and I loved that I had all that information at my fingertips. Whenever people came over and asked me questions about food, I'd run to this book and look things up to pretend I knew what I was talking about. I loved reading the descriptions of sauces and examining the amazing little engravings, like an etching of a live woodcock, a tiny, delicious game bird—who would have known what it looked like? I was fascinated by the process of French cooking, but the book showed, too, that food is about *more* than cooking; it's about geography, history, agriculture, tradition, art, anthropology—and nature, of course. It's something very sophisticated and deep; it's about culture, and I had a huge curiosity about it. I still do.

I started going to the new Williams-Sonoma store on Sutter Street in San Francisco. I was very interested in their rarefied cooking tools, things I had never seen before like melon ballers and lemon zesters. And they were the only things in the store I could afford to buy! Aesthetically, that store was fantastic. They had real French linens, and brown terrines with lids designed to look like the animal that was meant to be cooked inside: a green-headed mallard molded and painted for a duck terrine, a quail atop a quail terrine. And probably a little tiny one for a woodcock.

The supermarkets of the mid- to late 1960s were all about frozen foods and canned goods—the exact opposite of the French markets, and I figured out pretty swiftly that they were to be avoided if at all possible. Instead, I went to the Berkeley co-ops where we bought things in bulk, or I traveled to smaller specialty shops for particular foods. For charcuterie, Sara and I would go to Marcel et Henri in San Francisco, an old French place at Pacific and Polk Streets where we would get pâtés and *saucissons*. I also went a lot to the old Italian delicatessens in Oakland, like Genova Delicatessen, where we got olive oil, big long loaves of fresh Italian bread, olives that weren't the tired green ones stuffed with pimientos, and hunks of Parmesan cheese that the deli workers would cut off of their big wheels. I got to know all those guys from Italy behind the counter, older men around forty-five or fifty years old. When I approached the counter, it always sort of felt like *Here she comes!* I was *so* interested in what they had, and I was full of questions for them. They'd give me little samples to taste: "You like those olives? Try these, too! Here, have these breadsticks!" It was a mutual flirtation. It always smelled good in the deli—we'd pick up sandwiches before we left, the sorts where they'd layer in all the different cured Italian meats and a little pickled *giardiniera*.

Monterey Market was the best place in Berkeley for vegetables—but even so, there wasn't a lot of variety. The produce I was buying at the time was limited to potatoes,

carrots, and parsley, or heads of romaine lettuce that I'd
pull apart, keeping and eating only the tender hearts. I
could occasionally find small onions that would pass mus-
ter, and sometimes I'd buy Kentucky Wonder green beans,
throw out the big ones, and pretend I had haricots verts. I
was obsessed with haricots verts, the little skinny ones they
had in France. It was a texture thing for me—a green bean
salad married so much better when you were using the little
slender beans that took the dressing so well. It wasn't until
the mid-1970s, when a French friend of mine went to the
Chino ranch outside San Diego and sent me back a big box
of them, that I finally had real haricots verts in the United
States—I couldn't believe it.

At the co-op on Shattuck Avenue, up the street from our
house, we'd get rice and raisins and nuts, because the co-op
was the least expensive place to get staples in bulk. You had
to become a member—you'd buy a card for a nominal fee to
get in, and that gave you access to shop there. My mother
later bought me an investment plan through the co-op;
health food believer that she was, she loved that co-op. It
was organic, it did have that going for it, but the produce always felt overgrown and wilted, piled haphazardly in a dusty
bin, with no presentation like you'd find in a French shop. It
didn't excite me to cook with those vegetables: tired lettuce,
limp carrots. And the store smelled a little bad, sort of like
vitamin powder and bad incense.

Even though I shared a lot of counterculture values, I never connected with the hippie culture of the late 1960s, no question about it. The food in particular. I didn't really have friends who were hippies, either—except maybe my sisters Laura and Susan—because I was seeking out people who thought about food and culture in a different way. I didn't want anything to do with the hippies' style of health food cooking: a jumble of chopped vegetables tossed together with pasta—throw in a few bamboo shoots, and call it a Chinese meal. To me, that world was all about stale, dry brown bread and an indiscriminate way of eating cross-legged on couches or on the ground with none of the formality of the table. There was an aesthetic demarcation between the hippies and me, certainly as far as the food was concerned; I thought their approach was absolutely uncivilized, unrefined.

It's funny, because we came from the same philosophical counterculture place—we felt the same way about the war, the corruption of the powers that be, and sexual liberation—but we had different approaches for getting there. And there was sometimes a pushing away of intellectualism in the hippie culture. It felt to me like they were fighting for the freedom to completely disengage from society. "Let's live on the land out here—let's start a commune!" Perhaps they weren't, but that's how it felt, and that wasn't me. I thought the way to change was by engaging with society, and I believed in formality and beauty and deliberation. My friends and I valued a European aesthetic that was at odds with the Summer of Love aesthetic. You were either a beatnik or a hippie; I was more in the beat place, in the intellectual place. And I never smoked dope, that was a defining thing for me—it felt like dropping out (although wine was a different story). I couldn't drop out, I was an activist. But I was a sensualist, too.

Communal living was a big part of counterculture life in Berkeley then—and that was something I did embrace. David was good friends with the people running the *San Francisco Express Times* and was a little involved in layout and design, so most nights the staff would come over to our house and talk about the paper around our big dining room table, and I'd cook for everyone. A set of values in Berkeley at the time encouraged you to live in a certain way: you shared your bike, you picked people up in your car, you took them where they needed to go. People were always stopping by without invitations, and we took them all in: David Marowitz, Marvin Garson, Bob Novak, Richard Borovitz. It was almost all guys, printers and writers and artists. They certainly weren't helping me out in the kitchen, but I had free rein to cook whatever I liked, and I could see how happy the food made them. And they encouraged me—they gave me such praise, I wanted to make more dinners for them. When you have an appreciative audience like that, you want to keep going.

Luciano Delia, a friend of David's, would have us over for dinner at his house from time to time. He was Italian, a

great cook who would keep going into his kitchen and finding new foods to delight us, bringing things out like candied
orange rinds and a special coffee made from some rare bean
from Africa. I loved to do that, too, when people came to
our house: "Oh, just let me get *this* little taste for you. And
have you ever had *that*?" I wanted to keep people going, keep
them excited. David said the pleasure I took in entertaining
our friends was obvious; every single night I was putting
together these big meals, and at some point I thought, *You
know, I really enjoy cooking for other people.* When other people
liked my food, it was a huge satisfaction—my reaction was
just: *Oh my God! I can do this! I want to do it again!* I wanted to
live that life—except I was kind of going broke cooking for
them. I thought, *Hey, if I opened a restaurant, I could keep doing
this, but they'd have to pay.* I think that was when I had my first
vision about starting a restaurant of my own. I knew I could
do dinner parties, so I imagined I'd just double the size; instead of having ten people over for dinner at our house, I'd
have twenty people to my restaurant. We'd called my column
"Alice's Restaurant," so it *had* to have been on my mind. It
wasn't real yet—it was just a thought. But it was one thing
to cook for my starving friends—hungry and happy to eat
everything I cooked—and another to open a restaurant. I
knew that would be a big leap.

For a while when I was living with David, I was working
part-time as a waitress at the Quest, a little restaurant on

Shattuck Avenue between University and Hearst, down the street from where Chez Panisse would be, if you can believe it. You had just a couple of choices on the menu, with one cook in the kitchen. The best part of the job was that the owner played classical music like Chopin and Schubert, so when I moved among the tables to serve people, I felt like I was dancing. The owner was very eccentric. I have no memory of applying for the job or why I chose that place, none. I needed the money, though, and by then I'd done enough waitressing to feel like I knew how to do it. What I remember most is floating around the room with Chopin and Schubert. I was in sync with it.

I have a vague memory of the owner in the kitchen all alone, that he cooked all the food by himself and maybe had one dishwasher—so perhaps that's where I dreamed up the idea that somehow it wouldn't be that hard to run a little place all by myself. The Quest was pretty sophisticated for its time, for sure, because who's going to listen to Chopin and have very limited choices on the menu? Which isn't to say that the food there inspired me very much—it didn't. It was usually a three-course meal, and the food was generally a sort of hearty stew, like *boeuf bourguignon* or coq au vin. But it was unrefined—nothing was cooked to order, it had always been prepared ahead. It was mostly college students who came.

*One of my favorite things, when Chez Panisse first opened, was to wait tables. I liked it, and I was a great waitress. I liked talking about the food with the people at the different tables, and I knew I could get anybody to eat anything—I was a good salesperson. I was energetic and into it and quick. One time in the first couple of years of Chez Panisse, our chef Jeremiah Tower wanted to try a recipe for salt cod cooked on the grill. He had bought some baccalà at the Italian market but neglected to soak it. Or maybe he soaked it a little— but he definitely didn't soak it enough! So he grilled it and said to me, "Alice, it's a little salty, but tell them to wash it down with some good red wine." Someone in the dining room did complain, and I blithely said, "Oh, but that's the way it's supposed to be! Wash it down with red wine!"*

*Then during the evening we realized that it was like jerky— salt cod jerky. But I believed Jeremiah was right—because he was so confident. And lots of times when you believe in that way, you can win people over in the dining room: "I'm sure you're going to like it! Just taste it! It's different." If someone had told me that with enough conviction, maybe I'd have thought it was just an acquired taste. But then again, anything washed down with enough red wine can work.*

David's best friends, Charles and Lindsey Shere, lived down the street from us. Charles was the music director for KPFA, the local radio station. David and I often went over to their house for dinner. Lindsey would make northern Italian dishes like lasagna, or roast chicken and salad, but her desserts were the main event. (She had allowed me to include one of her desserts in my "Alice's Restaurant" column, a beautiful apricot soufflé; one of Charles's recipes also made it in, a recipe—if you can call it that!—for "Peppered Toast.")

Lindsey was Italian, one of five girls, and was used to cooking for her family. She'd started baking at age nine, and for a time when she was a teenager, she cooked all the meals for her family. We eventually came to a comfortable arrangement where I'd cook dinner at our place, and afterward we'd walk down the block to Charles and Lindsey's house to eat dessert. I loved the Dobos torte she made: eight layers of genoise cake, each one spread with mocha buttercream frosting, the whole thing covered with bittersweet chocolate. Little slices of caramelized genoise fanned out on top of the cake, and chopped hazelnuts were carefully pressed into the chocolate frosting on the outside. It was breathtaking. David and Charles were getting a bit into wine then, and we would drink Sauternes with that Dobos torte—that was my introduction to Sauternes.

Lindsey and Charles were ten years older than me and had three children. It seemed to me that they really knew how to live. Their little house was packed with so many meticulously chosen things: pottery, art, and lots of books. It was a pleasure to lose yourself in them. They had a six-foot-tall freestanding sheet of plexiglass in their living room that was a copy of *The Bride Stripped Bare by Her Bachelors, Even* by Marcel Duchamp. And Charles's conceptual artworks were

Charles and Lindsey Shere with their daughter Giovanna.

all around the house. A painting of his above the fireplace was white on white, and I loved how it changed throughout the day; when the streetlight came on at night, the painting became illuminated, creating silhouettes and shadows of the trees outside.

Charles and Lindsey were way more involved than we were in contemporary culture—they were always going to museum exhibits and modern dance performances and concerts. David, by contrast, was a traditionalist—we both were. David had found his raison d'être—political, artistic, the whole thing—in William Morris, one of the most significant cultural figures of Victorian England. *That* was where David's interest lay—not so much in the art of the twentieth century. He and I both romanticized the past.

Charles and Lindsey were two of my closest friends, and they were beautiful themselves—they looked like they'd stepped out of a French New Wave film. While David and Charles played chess, they were always in deep philosophical conversations, debating what seemed to me ridiculous things, like which writers best expressed the spirit of the eighteenth century; the relative merits of communism versus socialism throughout history; the relative merits of Charles's Armagnac versus David's Monnet cognac. They could go on for hours until I couldn't stand it anymore and had to go to bed.

Sometimes we would have conversations around the dinner table about my hypothetical restaurant: "Wouldn't it be great to have this sort of restaurant in this neighborhood?" Just fantasizing, joking around. In my mind, Lindsey just *had* to come and create her desserts at this little French restaurant I was going to open. She would graciously agree, but it was never taken terribly seriously.

Lindsey and Charles and David and I listened to music in a purposeful way. You didn't have Bach on in the background: you put it on, sat down, and *listened* to Bach. Charles went on to be a great music critic and a composer and wrote very out-there contemporary music. He went through phases of admiration for a lot of avant-garde composers: he had a Steve Reich phase for a while, and liked Anton Webern and Milton Feldman. Most of all he loved John Cage. Truthfully, I never loved that type of music—I knew they were all revered, but as Charles pointed out, I didn't even like Berlioz!

*Marcel Duchamp and John Cage were Charles's two great loves. Lindsey and Charles once celebrated a big anniversary of theirs at the restaurant, and David designed the invitation as a riff on Duchamp: a spare, elegant line drawing of a naked woman, with the text for the invitation in the pubic hair. They loved it.*

*Charles was also a key instigator of a mid-1980s dinner at the restaurant in John Cage's honor. John Cage was an amateur mycologist and had very intentional ways of eating—he was on a macrobiotic diet, wouldn't eat bottom fish, and would eat only oily fishes high in omega-3s. So our chef at the time, Paul Bertolli, dreamed up a special menu that included a beautiful cranberry bean soup with wild mushrooms. Lindsey and Charles were there in the dining room, of course. John Cage was in his early seventies, wide-eyed and frail, but he had a very deep voice and a great quiet presence; his partner, the dancer and choreographer Merce Cunningham, came with him. It was a fabulous night. Paul had even contacted a timpanist in the Los Angeles Philharmonic, who sent up a score to be played with kitchen implements, and Paul conducted all the cooks in a little kitchen concert, performed with pots and pans and whisks and wooden spoons.*

DECEMBER 4, 1967

*Dear Mother, Dad, and Suey,*

*I finally got things off to Ellen and Richie . . . It makes me so mad that they're over there that I can't write letters without becoming obnoxious. I haven't heard back from Richie although I have heard from his family who assures me that he is ok. I can only imagine what's going on in there. . . .*

*My desire to go to France has been rekindled upon meeting a French couple in Berkeley. We are going to eat dinner together often and speak French. At last! A real French tutor all to myself. It probably won't help, but the girl, Martine, speaks English about as well as I do French—which is not at all.*

I thought a lot about my imaginary little French bistro, and that meant I thought a lot about France. And because I missed the way things were over there, I sought out French friends. David and I met Claude and Martine Labro because Martine was a graphic artist who had connected with David; her husband was a graduate student at the university, doing research in applied mathematics. When we first met them, Martine didn't speak any English. We had many, many dinners over at Claude and Martine's—it was like being back in France. And we would have them over to our place, and I'd

try to impress them with my cooking. Meeting them really validated for me that it was all about France—Martine was such an aesthete. David was entranced by her as well—the red-haired woman on the very first poster of Chez Panisse was based on Martine.

Martine had an enormous aesthetic influence on me. The lighting at their house was always divine, and she was a great collector of antiques. We never cooked together, because Martine always had it all her own way—which was a *very* particular way. She was an artist, a painter, and lots

of times her canvas was the table—she always wanted it to look just *so*, and she wanted it all to be delicious. She was the quintessential table-setter. She found exquisite dishes at flea markets, like old chipped Limoges, and laid out big white linen napkins that covered your whole lap, put garden roses in vases, and adorned the table with hundred-year-old Provençal pitchers she'd brought with her from France.

Martine expanded my floral education. I knew about flowers from my childhood, and I had noticed flowers on tables in France but not very consciously—I'd just think,

*That table looks really pretty*. Near the gigantic flower market in Paris, little made-up bouquets of violets were for sale in the springtime, and I'd always buy one of them, a tight little bouquet that would cost a franc, and that was about all I could afford.

But it wasn't until I met Martine that flowers really became part of my domestic life—where the bouquet was an essential element of a room's decoration. It brought nature to the table, a connection to the world outside. She would place anemones, ranunculus, pansies, and scabiosas in beautiful vases, and she would paint the still lifes she had created. Martine had grown up partly in Burgundy, in the village of Gevrey-Chambertin, and partly in the South of France near Vence, where they make perfume from a type of rose called the Tango rose. Years later, when Martine and Claude moved back to Vence, there were Tango roses all over the markets. She would get armfuls of these peach-colored roses and put them in every room in the house. There was always a beautiful fragrant bouquet by my bed.

Do I think if something's beautiful, it's perfect? I guess you could say that. If I'm in a rapture of beauty, it's perfect to me.

Martine had no money—she and Claude never had any money—but she could always make something out of nothing. She knew how to make dinner special without having a giant steak on the table. She would buy a single chicken for ten people—I would have bought three!—but provided enough beautiful vegetables and side dishes on the plate that nobody ever missed it. It was quality over quantity, with lots of little courses. She was always concocting things from scratch that made the meal special: chicken liver pâtés, orange marmalade, incredible flat tarts with plums, and candied citrus peel. Martine's salads were amazing, too. She grew the lettuce in her backyard, and she had a little herb garden, with parsley and mint and chives, and she would go out, pick it, carefully wash the lettuce and herbs and roll them up in a towel to dry, then serve the leaves with anchovy dressing. The aliveness of something that had just been picked transformed the dish.

*After the restaurant had been open for a few years, people who lived in the neighborhood heard that we would trade fruits and vegetables from their gardens for a free lunch or dinner. I was forever on the hunt for great ingredients, and I'd learned from Martine that those just-picked things from the backyard could be the best of all. It was under the table, obviously—the health department knew nothing about it, and it certainly wasn't allowed. But we were careful about the way we wrapped things, the way we put food away, the way we cooled the stock, and we fastidiously scraped down and scrubbed the wooden counters many times a day. We didn't need a health inspector to come by and cite us in order to get us to maintain cleanliness—we did it on our own initiative.*

*It started when someone brought us French breakfast radishes from her garden. Those radishes were so good, we served them just*

*with butter and salt. Then we started getting Meyer lemons from peo-*
*ple's backyard trees. That got us into a whole era of Meyer lemon ice*
*cream and Meyer lemon sherbet; we'd put a scoop of each in a bowl,*
*juxtaposing the two subtly different textures, and that became one of*
*the most classic Chez Panisse desserts. A bit later on, a Latvian play-*
*wright, Juris Svendsen, became our first wild mushroom forager.*

*One time a German couple came into the kitchen when I was*
*cooking and brought in a handful—really, a handful—of finger-*
*ling potatoes. "This is a very special potato in Germany," they said.*
*"We'd like to trade it for a meal."*

*I looked at this tiny pile of long, strange, skinny little things*
*that would later become my favorite potato. I accepted them—how*
*could you not?—and sat the couple down for lunch.*

Every once in a long while, David and I would save up our
money and treat ourselves to dinner at one of the few French
restaurants in the area—but because Martine's dinners were
so good, the experience often left much to be desired. One
time Claude and Martine and David and I all went to Rue
Lepic, a French spot in San Francisco, and they refused to let
us in because Claude wasn't wearing a tie. Well, Claude was
immaculately dressed but didn't have a tie, and David did
happen to have a tie on, but he looked like a typical rumpled
intellectual from Berkeley. But they wouldn't budge: no tie,
no service. On our way out Claude called back to the maître
d', "Don't you know Rue Lepic is a street of whores?" They
were infuriated.

Martine's thriftiness was amazing. She went to the flea market every week, and I started tagging along. I couldn't distinguish the bad from the good, but she'd pick up treasures for nothing: linen napkins with monograms, little salt shakers, old engraved silver spoons, vases. I'd go with her and her stylish friend Jacqui West, and the two of them would ferret out the really great things at the market; in one phase they were collecting old patchwork quilts from the turn of the century. Once I did unearth a quilt for ten dollars that impressed the hell out of them, but they were the ones who really had the eye and the patience—whereas I had neither.

Jacqui and Martine were also looking for vintage clothes because they didn't cost anything and were so much more beautiful than new clothes. The clothes were very 1920s— drop-waisted and elegant, with tiny beading. Martine and Jacqui helped me appreciate what was special about those clothes and textiles. They got me to notice the incredible handiwork of, say, a vintage linen sheet that had been painstakingly embroidered. Lots of times when you look at clothing, you just don't see the person who made it. But my God, it could take someone years to do the embroidery on a single dress or create one of those patchwork quilts.

It's so great when someone you admire draws your attention to something, and suddenly you *see* it for the first time. Sometimes you need a friend who has great taste to help you to see that something has value and beauty. That's what Martine did for me—and Jacqui, too.

*Once Chez Panisse opened, I'd shop for clothes at a store in Oakland called Bizarre Bazaar, which was all vintage. In those heady years I was buying clothes that matched whatever the dinner was! I had my black truffle dress and my oyster dress. I'd walk in and say, "We're having such-and-such for dinner tonight," and Karen, the owner, would bring out everything: shoes, a purse, earrings, necklaces, a hat, the whole outfit. They were always on the verge of falling apart, because the clothes were silk and fragile and old, but I wore them like uniforms—I really worked in them.*

*A little later on Jacqui West opened a clothing store next door to Chez Panisse; she was in love with the restaurant and was determined to dress me. Her store, called La De Da, was very simple, full of all-cotton everyday clothing that had a French feel, with lots of stripes. She also sold Chinese slippers, which I've worn ever since. Once she had Martine wear a form-fitting dress that had dark purple and dark orange stripes and went all the way down to her ankles—Martine always cooked in that outfit, with her clogs and her curly auburn hair, and looked amazing. We were some of the first people Jacqui dressed; she later moved to Los Angeles and became a famous costume designer for movies, and now she's dressing Tilda Swinton and Leonardo DiCaprio in furs.*

Martine would tell me things the way they were; she'd give me criticisms about how I acted or cooked, and I'd be able to hear them and say, "Okay, that's right." She could point out that I was impatient and didn't want to take the time to do things thoroughly—she'd note that I hadn't washed the lettuce well enough, or that I'd picked all the lettuce she was growing and destroyed the look of the garden, or that I wasn't paying attention to cleaning up after myself. I was both extravagant and impatient. And Martine was very definitive—loving, but definitive: "Alice, you bought too much meat. We're never going to eat all that." Or "You slice the tart *this* way." Or "*This* is the dish we serve the chicken on." There was never a question in it, just—*this* is the way it is. And that sort of criticism wakes you up. When you're being critiqued on your work, whether that work is assembling a tart or boning out a leg of lamb, you *cannot* take it personally. If you do, it makes it impossible to have a good conversation.

*If I really like and admire somebody I'm working with at the restaurant, it's not difficult to just say, "Whoa! That wasn't quite right, was it?" And usually they'll say, "No, it probably wasn't." Very occasionally there's resistance, and I'll have to say, "Well, I don't think it's right, period." But that happens very rarely these days. I hope everybody can see that I have a valuable role as a critic, because I've been there since the beginning, and I've seen the restaurant go through lots of changes. And I'm constantly learning about food, and I'm out in the restaurant world all the time. I'm also in the dining room of our own restaurant all the time. Because I've worked in both the dining room and the kitchen, I do know what*

*I'm asking for. I think it's unusual for an owner of a restaurant to have worked in both places.*

*It bothers me when people at the restaurant don't ask for my opinion. I joke that I think of myself as an amazing resource! Sometimes I think people don't want to ask because I can be so definitive, or dictatorial, but I've learned through the years, I hope, to be more polite and more understanding with people in the kitchen. I learned that from my father, really—that you need to first tell somebody something good about what they're doing, then tell them what they need to do to improve.*

*I've never been as open to criticism as I want to be—though I try. It's hard to hear. Many times I've received criticisms in ways that have helped me, though—saved me, even. The first time I ever went to New York to cook was in 1979, when I was invited to be part of a big event at Tavern on the Green showcasing two young chefs from the United States and two from France. That's when I met Paul Prudhomme, the other American chef. At that point, Paul was writing cookbooks and running his famous restaurant in New Orleans, K-Paul's Louisiana Kitchen. He was incredible—such a big and jolly man, so friendly. I went to the meal he'd prepared, and he served a dessert that was really extraordinary in my life. He'd made a perfect little replica of a Cajun cottage out of chocolate—with a tiny front porch on it and everything—for each person. The servers came by with a bowl of warm crème anglaise and poured it over the roof; the chocolate house melted and these incredible strawberries came tumbling out from inside the cottage. They were Louisiana strawberries, with a very different shape, smaller and more elon-*

*gated than the typical strawberries. They almost tasted like fraises des bois. It was an astonishing dish.*

*The next day was our day to make lunch: my sous-chef was Jean-Pierre Moullé, who would later become the downstairs chef of Chez Panisse. It was just the two of us—he and I had come across the country on Easter Sunday with an entire spring lamb as our checked luggage. I also brought a box of lettuce still planted in dirt—that was my carry-on—because I wanted to wait until the last possible moment before our meal to pick it.*

*At eight that morning we walked into Tavern on the Green, me with the lettuce growing in soil, and Jean-Pierre with a whole spring lamb that was yet to be butchered slung over his shoulder. At first it didn't occur to me that Jean-Pierre and I needed help. The two of us would be cooking for one hundred people, but somehow I thought we could do it on our own!*

*We felt dwarfed by that kitchen. I was afraid to put anything in the refrigerator—I was positive that my food would get lost in there. Somebody was on the loudspeaker: "Table two in room three, pick up!" like an air traffic controller. There was a stainless steel salad spinner four feet in diameter, an electric thing where you pressed a button, and it whizzed around and rinsed all the salad. I was sure it was going to crush all my little baby lettuces.*

*Paul Prudhomme came by to see us and asked very kindly, "Alice, do you need help?"*

*I said something to the effect of "Oh no, we're okay."*

*"Well, I'm a little worried about you, Alice," he said. "You might not have enough time. What are you doing today?"*

"We're opening oysters on the half shell," I said. "And we're doing whole baked garlic, spring lamb on the grill, and a dessert." I wanted it to sound convincing, like I knew what I was doing.

Then Paul just took charge, shouting orders to his team of seventeen cooks: "Let's have two people on oysters! Two people on the terrace to start the fire! The rest can help JP bone the lamb!"

I just thought, WHAT? We're not ready! I felt like a fool—here we were, just two cooks, and he had brought seventeen people with him to do his meal. But I'm so glad I heard him and let down my pride enough to accept his help. I am indebted to him to this day. He saved us, and it taught me enormously—I felt like a kid from the country. Jean-Pierre knew a whole lot about putting together something like that, but I knew nothing about cooking a big menu in someone else's kitchen. And then Paul came in and just organized everything. And the greatest part was that although we were creating meals alongside really famous French chefs, the next day the Times talked only about the meals we two American chefs had created. I wrote Paul many love letters over the years—he was such a soulful person, and I really miss him.

# CHAPTER 9

# Learning by Doing

My sister Ellen's friend Barb Carlitz was a Montessori teacher, and after I graduated from Berkeley in 1967, she told me about Montessori. Like most people in the world, I had no idea what I was going to do after I graduated. To support myself, I was waitressing at the Quest, and I worked for a time at Diablo Press next door to David's shop, taking inventory and wrapping packages. I loved cooking at home and was doing the "Alice's Restaurant" column with David. I had my fantasy of a little French bistro, but it never felt like a real way to support myself in the moment.

And so while all that was going on, I was finding out more about Montessori. I was fascinated by the philosophy; it reminded me of what had worked so well in Mrs. Mead's class when I was in third grade, and how much I had loved her sensitive, hands-on approach to teaching. I could never learn in the abstract, and Montessori was all about learning through your senses, learning by doing; when students were

doing math, for example, they would lay out these beautiful wooden blocks, so the students could see and feel exactly what they were measuring. That method of teaching completely appealed to me. All the Montessori materials were so beautiful—they were made in Holland out of real wood and real glass.

One of the first things I responded to about Montessori was the fact that there were lots of games you played that employed food—they had smelling canisters, for example, and you had to match up the scent with the food or herb or spice. Or you would reach your hand into a bag filled with a real fruit or vegetable, and you'd try to guess what it was from the feel of it. They had exercises with taste, too—you'd taste something sour and have to identify it as a lemon. Montessori education felt like a school reform movement—learning through the senses was a countercultural idea, too. It felt like a hopeful way to enact change.

There was a Montessori school down the block from me on Francisco Street, and I started helping out there as an intern. After about a year of assisting there on and off, I thought I should get formal training, so I applied to the international Montessori training school in London, for a nine-month certification program that would allow me to open a Montessori school anywhere in the world. I was accepted.

It was a big decision to go to London in October 1968—I don't know how I made some of these decisions!—but I talked to my parents about it, discussed it with David, and made the leap. I think I was looking for a way to get back to Europe, and David told me he would meet me there and stay in England for several months after I got settled. The Montessori teachers' program was up in Hampstead, about a half an hour north of London's city center, and students attended from all over the world, more women than men.

When I reread the letters I sent my mother from Hampstead, it seemed that yes, I was busy there. The work wasn't hard, but it was detailed and time-consuming. We had to learn puzzles, going from the very simple to the very complex, like putting together a map of the whole world. I had to make a scrapbook of leaves, identifying each leaf and tracing around the outside so I'd learn all the local trees of Hampstead. I had to calligraph that book, too—Montessori was also about handwriting, and I was fascinated to do that for my scrapbook.

I had a leg up in that department already, because David had been teaching me calligraphy; he thought I had beautiful handwriting (though, of course, he was a biased party). People always thought I had nice penmanship when I was a kid, for whatever that's worth. I do think that people notice when your handwriting is good—it's a lost art in this country, and nobody knows how to write well. Writing longhand takes time—as Maria Montessori said, the hand is the instrument of the mind. You can do calligraphy without a calligraphy pen—even with a ballpoint pen, if you want to—

but you have to practice endlessly to get it right. I would do *A*'s over and over again, working on lined paper so I'd get the right proportions each time. And yes, once I had seen perfectly calligraphed pages and started attempting to reproduce that myself, I felt that the way I'd been writing all those years was utterly unpolished. To this day, I really like it when people in my office take calligraphy—I want everyone to understand my obsession. I think the way you write to someone tells them how much you care about them.

Maria Montessori had originally trained as a doctor and examined the development of children's motor skills, designing equipment to help fine-tune them. A Montessori school is about educating the whole child—that spoke to me. Maria Montessori talked a lot about how zero to six years is such a formative age for a child. She broke it down into two stages, zero to three and three to six. From zero to three years, children are really just absorbing things like little sponges, and from three to six they begin to use those skills. Maria Montessori felt there was a parallel between education and *The Divine Comedy*. You start in the hell of not knowing anything, and then Virgil—your teacher—guides you through purgatory. Once you ascend to paradise, to the place of knowledge, the teacher doesn't need to be there anymore. When all the senses are educated and empowered, Maria Montessori said, every child discovers something he or she can do that's amazing; after they find that thing, they're in *paradiso*. Every child has something incredible to contribute. I've thought of

that in the restaurant every day since it opened—that someone who's not good *here* might be really good over *there*. He or
she just hasn't found the right calling yet.

Preparing the classroom in a seductive way is a crucial
part of the Montessori method. I loved that. The idea is to
make the classroom *so* inviting that the kids come into it and
immediately want to explore. That's why there's beautiful
equipment, flowers in vases, little chairs and tables that are
always taken care of, repainted whenever they get worn. The
children help clean things and fix them again as a way of seeing what their work is about. Making things look and feel
beautiful is so important to Montessori pedagogy. It shows
that you care. In the same way later on, I wanted Chez Panisse to be enticing to people from the moment they walked
through the front door—I wanted to awaken all their senses,
and I *especially* wanted it to smell good. I wanted it to be
about the aroma of rosemary, of bread baking, of the wood
oven—those are the ways to reach people subconsciously.

*When we built the Edible Schoolyard kitchen in 1995, a kitchen
classroom at Martin Luther King Jr. Middle School in Berkeley, we
made very conscious choices about everything we put in the room—
just as Maria Montessori had, and just as Martine and Aunt Ina
had done with their homes. We were given one of those low-slung,
charmless portable buildings to work with, so we started by taking
out all of the partitions to make one large room with as much natural light as possible. And then we got artists involved in the design.*

San Francisco artist and designer Buddy Rhodes created polished gray-green concrete countertops, which we turned into big worktables with beautiful sturdy wooden legs. We made cabinets where you could see everything on the shelves: mortars and pestles, stacks of dishes, water glasses, pitchers. Right before we opened, we had a kitchen-warming and asked everyone to bring something for the kitchen that was made out of wood. We got lots of butcher boards and wooden spoons, of course, but we also got an enormous wooden mortar and pestle from Thailand, an heirloom from someone's family. It's still a treasured possession in the kitchen.

We make sure that there are always flowers on the tables, and that all the knives and kitchen tools are laid out neatly in a wooden box. And we always have a little site near the entrance, almost like an altar, where all the vegetables and fruits of the moment are arranged beautifully. I wanted it to be a space where the kids would fall in love from the moment they entered. And in fact, the students often come back later in the afternoon just to do their homework or play the old piano that we put in a corner. When kids walk into the room, they know right away that something special and beautiful has been arranged for them. You don't have to say a word, they just know it instantly, and they know they're loved. It's why we say at the Edible Schoolyard that beauty is the language of care.

When I first arrived in Hampstead, I walked through the neighborhood looking for a place to stay. I saw a lovely old brick house that had a turret. I walked up to it, and a plaque by the door said MRS. WANDA'S HOUSE FOR GIRLS. I knocked and asked the woman if she had any rooms to let. I was crushed when she said no, it was full.

"I'd love to live up there in that turret!" I told her. It reminded me of the turret in David's house, and I thought he would like it when he came.

"Nobody's staying up in the turret," she said, "but I don't want to rent that out because it doesn't have any heating." I told her it didn't matter, I wanted that turret no matter what, so she showed it to me and I rented it for something like seven pounds a week. It had a minuscule bedroom, a little sitting room, and the tiniest kitchen you've ever seen. I could just barely stand in it. It had a tiny little enameled-front stove—just two burners and a broiler, with no proper oven at all—and a sink.

But I've always liked a challenge, so I'd often have a couple of people over for little dinner parties, doing lots of French cooking, usually from Elizabeth David's books—I steamed mussels, and I actually managed to make some half-decent tarts in that tiny broiler, though I'm not entirely sure how. It was very cold all that winter, and you had to bring the electric space heater everywhere you went and put coins in it to get it to operate. But when you cooked in the kitchen, it would get warm and the window would steam up until condensation dripped down the panes.

*I love mussels: I used to eat heaping piles of them when I was in France and England, steamed open with a little white wine and butter and garlic. I ate them back home in California, too, but then fifteen years later, maybe in the mid-1990s, I got one that wasn't good—it wasn't bad, it was just off. Some time would pass, and then it would happen again. And again. The fourth time it happened, I said, "No, I can't do mussels anymore, they're too unpredictable." It was tragic, because I do love them. We stopped using mussels at Chez Panisse about ten years ago, because if you get a single bad one, it spoils the whole pot. I'm on the verge of saying that about clams, too.*

*I absolutely think the likelihood that you'll have a bad one is increasing; the pollution in the water is filtering through clams, mussels, shrimp, and oysters, and the sea is changing. You have to be so careful. And many, many people have allergies. I think it's all of a piece. The places where some companies are shrimping is shocking. Recently in Sardinia with my friends Bob and Tony, I indulged in mussels for the first time in years—I felt that the water was clean, and the mussels were from right there off the coast of Bosa, and we'd got them out of the water that day. But in general I'm just too worried—especially in the position of running the restaurant, I don't want to take a chance, ever.*

That winter in Hampstead it was *so* cold, and I'd stand *so* close to that pay-by-the-minute electric heater, that one night the whole back of my nightgown, a polyester thing, went up in flames. All of a sudden it just burned up and disappeared— one second it was there, and the next it wasn't. That could have been the end of Mrs. Wanda's turret.

·   ·   ·

I ate a lot of Indian food in London because it was afford-able. My sister Ellen's friend Barb Carlitz and her husband, Michael, were living out in Bolton Gardens in Kensington, and there was an Indian restaurant around the corner from them, the Star of India, where we ate all the time. I got into biryanis with the fried onions scattered on top, yogurt *raita*, and lamb *rogan josh*. I'd have all that with a Pimm's Cup—that was the British colonial influence for you. And when I was in school, I went to a nearby Indian restaurant every day and had a prawn and spinach curry for lunch.

*Recently I went back to Hampstead with my friend Inigo to see if the restaurant was still there—I couldn't believe it, I remembered exactly the road to go to, Lyndhurst Terrace. I found the house with the turret where I'd lived, and then we started looking for the Indian restaurant on the nearby streets. We found one that didn't look familiar, but it had a banner on top saying* OPEN MORE THAN FIFTY YEARS! *so I figured it had to be my restaurant. We went in and were the only people there. I still didn't recognize anything, but they served us in the same incredibly hospitable way: bringing hot plates to the table, taking off the little covers of fragrant dishes as they presented them, folding napkins really nicely. It was wonder-fully elegant service, even in the simplest place.*

*Not long after Chez Panisse opened, I went to a class with Madhur Jaffrey at Gene Opton's house. Madhur had just published her first book,* An Invitation to Indian Cooking, *and she made puris—these little whole wheat flatbreads you roll out thinly and*

*put in hot oil, and they puff up into airy little balloons, like magic.*
*I was astonished by the alchemy. I came home and re-created them*
*right away. She also taught us how to make rice—where you steam*
*it, drizzle the saffron over the top, then finish it by baking in the*
*oven. That was probably my first real encounter with making rice—I*
*didn't know how before then. Our family didn't have rice often when*
*I was little—maybe Uncle Ben's every once in a while. But this In-*
*dian way, with long-grain basmati and the fragrance of the rice with*
*the saffron, was so special. I made rice like that for years.*

*I've had a connection to Indian food my whole life—and it*
*helps that I've had extraordinary teachers like Madhur Jaffrey and*
*Niloufer Ichaporia King to educate and inspire me about it. I love*
*the aromas: the sizzling spices on the stove, the steaming basmati*
*rice, the smell of the fire and the tandoor. I like pairing the spicy with*
*something cool, like raita, and having lots of little courses, where*
*you can taste something sweet like a chutney or something sour like*
*a pickle. You can adjust all the flavors to your own personal taste.*
*There's beauty in the way it looks, too, that's very much in my color*
*palette: maroons, saffrons, earth-bound colors. Indian cooking is a*
*comfort food for me, and I think it all goes back to England and feel-*
*ing comfortable being by myself. That's how I feel these days at the In-*
*dian restaurant around the corner from me in Berkeley—I'll go there*
*to eat alone, and they'll always take care of me and find something*
*I'll really like: whole wheat puris, tandoori chicken, the tastiest dal.*

London in 1968 was a trip; like Berkeley, it was in the midst
of a cultural shift. Antonioni's *Blow-Up* had come out a

couple years before, and music and fashion were changing every two minutes: there were the mods, the rockers, all of it. Biba was *the* hip spot in London at the time for women's fashion; it had miniskirts and dresses with Art Nouveau prints, the stuff that Twiggy was wearing, and I'd sneak off there and buy short-short skirts when I could scrape together the money. Afterward I'd eat in the ethnic restaurants on Barrow Street—there was a Greek restaurant where we'd have shish kebabs at a little counter.

And London had another delicious part, too: it was a time of black currant ice cream and sole Véronique at Rules restaurant. I'd never before tasted anything like Dover sole. At Rules, they served a whole sole, filleted in a beurre blanc with peeled grapes. I don't know how I saved up enough money to eat that—I probably begged my parents. I felt very connected to all the ingredients in these places in London; the fish, the mussels, the oysters on the half shell were all astonishing. It reminded me of France, and I was so surprised and delighted.

I often spent time wandering around Harrods Food Hall; it was much too expensive for me, but I went there to look. They had all the French cheeses I loved, wild game hung from the ceiling in the fall, amazing tiled walls adorned with scenes of pheasants—it all knocked me out. I also went to Elizabeth David's cookware shop in Pimlico a lot, near Sloane Square. It took me about an hour to get there because I was way up north. Elizabeth David was usually there, but I was much too shy to introduce myself. She was very elegant and kept to herself—behind the counter, her hair swept back, wearing a white blouse and tan sweater, sorting and arranging her things. I didn't want to break her concentration; she was busy. She made beautiful window displays—white French terrines and gratin dishes, glass decanters, footed cake stands, mortars and pestles, towers of red currant Bar-le-Duc preserves in multifaceted glass jars. And she had a little basement part of the shop with stacks of dishes on the floor, like brown crocks for making couscous. Everything was well chosen, all the linens and knives. I'd buy little things like a melon baller and the Bar-le-Duc jam, or I'd get her pamphlets on pickling or making preserves. But I was just too intimidated to say anything to her.

*I never imagined I'd meet Elizabeth David, but she did come to Chez Panisse much later, with Gerald Asher, a writer for* Gourmet *magazine. We prepared a special dinner for her at the restaurant, but my real obsession was making a picnic for her: she and Gerald were on their way to Yosemite, so I volunteered to assemble a picnic basket for her to take for lunch. I went to my favorite antique shop and bought Early American glasses and dishes I knew she would appreciate, things that I could imagine seeing in her store: two ancient wineglasses, the old heavy kinds, vintage linens, and a patchwork quilt for the two of them to sit on. I spent way too much money, and it was heavy—especially with two bottles of wine! They had thought they were getting a bagged lunch, and this picnic basket was gigantic. But I wanted her to feel like it was really a picnic from California. They loved it, and she took all the glasses and linens back to England.*

I wrote postcards to Lindsey and Charles from London, telling them about the concerts I was seeing, the art exhibits, and my cold but very romantic little turret. I wrote my parents and my sisters, too, but those letters were longer, more involved, and usually included requests for money. But I put a lot of thought into those postcards to Lindsey and Charles; I wanted to write really good notes to them about all the sights that I knew would interest them, with images on the fronts that they would really love.

*I've always loved postcards, both sending them and getting them. I really believe that the right picture on a postcard tells it all. Plus you don't have to write too much on the back! I felt I could write a few lines, and the picture on the front could convey everything I couldn't express. I have boxes and boxes of postcards I've collected over the years—I buy them and send them off wherever I go but always come home with way more than I can send. And even in the places where I stay when I'm traveling, I'll take postcards I find and prop them up on shelves of the hotel room, in places that need a little temporary decoration and beauty. It's an inexpensive way to make a room beautiful.*

Shortly after I got to England, my friend Jon Cott came over to visit; I was secretly fascinated with him. He was a writer for *Rolling Stone* whom I'd met through Charles and Lindsey back in Berkeley, one of those brilliant people, a poet and music writer with dark eyes and curly hair and so much charm and magnetism. He interviewed some of the most amazing people on the planet. Jon sent me a postcard letting me know that he was traveling to London to hang out with John Lennon and interview him for *Rolling Stone*. He asked if I wanted to go to dinner with the two of them. I was *way* too overwhelmed by the prospect of sitting down with those two, so I said no thanks. Needless to say, I regret that one.

Toward the holidays that year, David came to stay for a few months. Mrs. Wanda had a rule of no men after eleven p.m., so despite my best efforts, David couldn't stay in my turret—he and I tried and failed to find another place to live together, so he ended up in a room by himself somewhere near Hampstead. David revered British art and literature and culture and wanted to visit all his touchstones, like the illuminated manuscripts in the British Museum and the antiquarian bookshops, and we went together to the William Morris Gallery along the Thames. We both adored William Morris: "Art must begin at home. Have nothing in your house that you do not believe to be useful, or believe to be beautiful." I recently went back to the gallery again. All I had seen the first time were Morris's beautiful wallpapers and his amazing designs; this time all I saw were his politics—

William Morris was a tremendously influential figure in the early socialist movement in England.

David and I were immersed in England, but that didn't mean we were oblivious to what was happening politically back in the United States. There was no way to ignore it. What was taking place in Vietnam was increasingly awful. The war seemed to be just getting bigger, wreaking more and more havoc in Southeast Asia, threatening to take our friends away—threatening to take David away.

DECEMBER 1968

*Dear Mother, Dad, Laura, Ellen, Bob and Little David (is it fair to include all these people so I only write one letter?)*

*Well, first of all another disaster of sorts—David was just classified 1A by the army and they denied him permission to leave the country. This means he has 60 days to appeal, which he is doing just now vis-à-vis Berkeley lawyers, etc. It's almost certain he'll be drafted shortly. We're waiting to hear from the lawyer so we aren't pessimistic yet. God, wouldn't it be awful if he had to return or couldn't get his visa extended. . . .*

*I'm getting very nervous about the wedding but excited at the same time. It seems such a big decision to have made in such a short time. Does everyone feel like this? I can't wait to see you, Mother.*

I almost married David while I was in London. We had been loosely engaged before I left Berkeley—we lived together, and an engagement seemed like the obvious next step—and we spontaneously decided to get married in England after Christmas, on Aunt Ina's birthday, January 7. Our parents were coming over and everything. But in the weeks right before the date, we decided against it—even after I had bought my wedding dress, a long lavender silk gown from Biba. Getting married had seemed like the logical thing to do, because we did really care about each other. But when we walked right up to it, both of us realized it didn't feel right. We had the good sense to realize we weren't in love enough to get married.

Afterward we took a misbegotten trip to Paris. Despite everything we were going through, I had thought David would love France—because I loved France more than any place in the world. But he didn't. He didn't speak a word of French and was miserable the whole time—and so was I. He just wanted to go home to what was familiar to him. I was upset by that trip—in part, I think, because I was coming to the realization that there *was* something deeply different about the two of us (and not just because he didn't like France). He went home not long after that—thankfully, he wasn't drafted in the end—and it was a tearful goodbye.

It was incredibly sad—but I was relieved, too, because both of us felt this decision was the right one. I mean, you're talking about the person you want to spend the rest of your life with. I was always impulsive, and I think that's how we got all the way to that point—"Let's just get married! I'll get the dress at Biba!" That kind of thing. David was not impulsive himself, so I think the blame for the wedding that wasn't, if you can call it blame, rested with me. I didn't return to Berkeley for ten months or so, which gave the wound time to heal. We really loved each other, but we couldn't spend our whole lives together.

In the aftermath of our breakup, I tortured myself further still by reading John Keats—the ultimate romantic. I read a lot of Virginia Woolf and Vita Sackville-West then, too—I was totally into the Bloomsbury circle and the romance of England. I memorized my favorite Keats poem, "Ode to Autumn"—it felt like what I had experienced that fall in Hampstead, exactly that:

> Season of mists and mellow fruitfulness,
>     Close bosom-friend of the maturing sun;
> Conspiring with him how to load and bless
>     With fruit the vines that round the thatch-eaves run;
>         To bend with apples the moss'd cottage-trees,
>             And fill all fruit with ripeness to the core;
>                 To swell the gourd, and plump the hazel shells
>     With a sweet kernel; to set budding more,
>         And still more, later flowers for the bees,
>             Until they think warm days will never cease;
>                 For Summer has o'erbrimm'd their clammy cells.

The English countryside was so beautiful. I loved going to Hampstead Heath; when the daffodils came up that spring, the whole hillside was covered with thousands of *Narcissus poeticus*, with garnet red centers and white petals and an ethereal smell. I can smell it right now. I was enchanted by the gardens at Sissinghurst Castle, where Vita Sackville-West had lived. One weekend in April or May, I took a train to Kent, about three hours, and then a bus to Sissinghurst. It was just the type of place my mother and Aunt Ina would have loved, this crumbling Elizabethan estate with rambling roses climbing over the bricks, and I knew a lot of the plants there because of my mother. I saw an old orchard of apple and pear trees that was full of wild grasses and great drifts of those yellow daffodils with the little orange coronas. Other areas of the garden were so trimmed and orderly—it was a magical combination of wild and tamed.

I was tempted to go to Cornwall but didn't, because I'd been there briefly on a trip with Sara back in 1965, and it had just been too cold. And I didn't like the food there—I had been in a very French state of mind then, and I wanted no part of those meat-filled pastries, the dense ones with beef and potatoes, and the overly sweet desserts with clotted cream. We had gone into a Cornish tea shop, and none of the food there was any good. I never really got into tea while I was in England. I did enjoy the little tea cakes but never the whole afternoon tea ritual: to me, it was nothing more than uninteresting white bread sandwiches with very little flavor, and unnecessarily formal and expensive. Mind you, we went and had some afternoon teas in Harrods, but after my radicalization in Berkeley, its mannerisms and exclusiveness just felt like an upper-class tea trip.

For a short time, I had a job as a waitress in a pub on the other side of London, though it took me much too long to get there. One night at the pub, I met this tall, dark-haired handsome guy and really fell for him. I left with him that night and never went back to work! I don't think I called or even told the pub, I just never showed up. I've never done anything like that since. (The little interlude with that man was brief but very passionate.) But I learned one thing from that job: every day we had to take *every* bottle off the back bar, wipe it down, and put it back. I said, "*Why* are we doing this all the time?" And the pub owner said, "Because they never get dirty if you do it every single day." Later on we did that at Chez Panisse—and it's true, they never get dirty.

I was a waitress at another place in London after that: Conrad's Bistro. It had an upstairs and a downstairs. The people who worked there were paid very poorly, and to make up for it, they were always taking home things they weren't supposed to: food, wine, glasses, silverware, salt and pepper shakers. People who work in restaurants can do things like that, especially if there isn't an existing culture of *giving* them things. That influenced me a lot later on: we let people buy olive oil and vinegar and even silverware and glasses at cost through Chez Panisse—and gave some of those things away sometimes, too.

Right after school ended and I got my international Montessori certificate, I spent several months camping through Europe with a friend from the Montessori program, Judy Johnson, a tall brunette with a beautiful smile. Judy was game for anything. She and I were simpatico in a lot of ways, and she was very easy to be with—she was more courageous than I was about traveling and knew how to read a map. Judy and I bought a used Mini Cooper from a friend and decided to camp through Hungary, Bulgaria, Turkey, and Greece. I was madly reading Henry Miller's *The Colossus of Maroussi* at the time, so I was primed for Greece, and one of the Montessori teachers had a house in Corfu and had told us to come visit. I was thinking of Sachertortes, too, and how I wanted to eat them in the Hungarian pastry shops. Somehow I wasn't picturing the actual realities of the countries where we were going, just how I wanted to eat in particular places.

Jon Cott had told me about Bulgarian music, too, and would play me records of the hauntingly beautiful peasant music. And somehow I had found out they made rose perfume in Bulgaria, so I was imagining fragrant fields of maroon roses, as part of this incredible culture of singing and dancing and drinking. And, of course, when we pulled into Sofia, we found it was under Soviet rule. We were absolutely shocked; it was all new buildings of cement and concrete, no cafés, no life on the streets, no trees. I remember thinking, *We* have *to get out of here.* All those romantic visions of country-side and perfume and dancing were just gone. We drove into Yugoslavia and got very drunk on slivovitz, the plum brandy that is a regional specialty.

Judy and I had the same open attitude about sex—we were both pretty free-spirited. We didn't speak any of the languages in the countries we were visiting, but it didn't really make a difference. Somewhere along the way, at one of

the campsites where we were staying, I met a German guy, and he invited me to sneak off to his tent. I still know only two words in German: *langsam* and *schnell*.

At a Yugoslavian campsite, we met two French guys, Pierre and Richard, and decided to travel in tandem with them into Turkey. We had our Mini Cooper, and they had their Citröen Deux Chevaux. It was so fortunate that we found these male companions, because as single women, we never could have gone into restaurants by ourselves. We were just good friends, not dating, but Pierre and Richard became our de facto "husbands." Before we'd go into a town, Judy would get into the Deux Chevaux with Pierre, and Richard would climb into the Mini Cooper with me. The Turks didn't accept us any other way than as married couples.

*Women traveling alone often don't have an easy time of it. I first went to Italy in the mid-1970s, after the restaurant finally got on an even keel, and I needed a vacation. I met some friends in France and was planning to see others a little later in Italy, but I had a few weeks of free time in between. I felt so empowered then, running my own restaurant, that I figured I could just take off on a train and explore Europe by myself. I thought, Well, I'm just going to go to Italy, even though I didn't speak a word of Italian.*

*I took the train to Siena but hadn't arranged for a place to stay. So I went by myself from one hotel to another, and no one had any* rooms. By the time I reached the last hotel in town, I had tears in my eyes, and the manager said, "Well, there's a youth hostel down the way. You can have a room there, I'm sure." I found it, a high-ceilinged, gigantic place, with little cubicles cordoned off in this one big room. I got a bed but couldn't sleep that whole night—there was constant noise from people coming in, moving around, and talking. In the morning, I went downstairs to the room where they served breakfast and sat down by myself. Nobody waited on me—other people came in and got waited on, but not me. After a very long time, I said in English to this waiter, "If you don't wait on me, I'm going to go make my own cappuccino." (I was adept at cappuccinos from working the bar at Chez Panisse.) He still didn't pay me any mind, so I went over, made my cappuccino, put my money down, and left. I was so upset. I thought they were prejudiced against me because I didn't speak Italian.

Then I took the train to La Spezia. I planned to have lunch right near the train station and sat down at a café. Once again nobody waited on me! Again! No one would even acknowledge my exis-tence. At the hostel I had been angry, but now I was hurt—I just didn't understand. Then an Italian guy at the next table introduced himself and said, "I'm not trying to pick you up, but I just wanted to say—I've been watching what's happening. Do you know why they're ignoring you?"

"No, why?"

"Because you're a woman by yourself, and if you're eating by yourself, they assume you're a prostitute. Come with me to the place *next door, and we'll get some lunch." And as soon as I was sitting in the company of a man, like a "respectable" woman—then, of course, people acknowledged that I existed again.*

Somehow Judy and Pierre and Richard and I got our hands on some Lebanese hash in Turkey. The four of us were smoking it, driving down the beach road by the sand dunes, and we thought, *Why drive on the road? Let's just go drive over there on the sand!* We were going sixty miles an hour in our two ridiculous little cars, sliding down the dunes, laughing and laughing and laughing. All of a sudden, the Mini Cooper came to an abrupt stop—one of the tires was punctured. We had to camp right there on the sand dunes. The next morning the French guys took us into this little remote Turkish town to replace the tire. It took two days to get it fixed— the mechanics had no idea what the minuscule tire for the Mini Cooper was, and they certainly didn't have any replacements, so they basically had to sew the rubber together by hand. It took them forever.

One night we set up camp but didn't realize we were in somebody's pasture. We pitched our tents, and in the morning one of the shepherds had tucked a bowl of warm goat's milk inside the flap of the tent for us for breakfast. That hospitality and kindness from complete strangers astounded me—and the freshness and aliveness of the warm goat's milk was incredible. I'll never forget it.

We drove out to Cappadocia, right below Ankara, where they have those fairy castle rock formations. In a small town nearby, we met some people who said a wedding was going on, and they asked us if we would like to come. Astonished and flattered to be invited, we agreed; the boys and the girls were separated, and Judy and I joined the women's gathering. In a little room, women of all ages were painting the bride with henna. When we entered, they seated us on cushions in the middle of the room, and all of a sudden we

became more important than the bride! I was ashamed that we were the center of attention, but everyone was so happy that we'd joined the wedding party, that we were gracing their wedding as honored guests. Their hospitality was overwhelming. They played a beautiful stringed instrument and a tambourine, and the women danced in a circle for us. And then we danced with them—we were there for hours, dancing and decorating ourselves. Eventually the women carried the bride over to the men, who had been in their

own area, drinking and smoking and celebrating—it was a magical day.

The next day they took us to their school because they were touched by the fact that Judy and I were both school-teachers. The students wanted a picture with us and gave us a present of walnuts. They wanted to give us a parting gift for the road, and that's all they had—we discovered later that the walnuts were all dried out inside, but it didn't matter. They didn't want us to feel we were obliged to stick around or to give them something in return—never. They gave without any expectations. I don't think I'd ever felt that before in my whole life. When you can convey that to someone, it is a very rare gift.

We wound our way through Turkey with the guys, went south to swim in the Aegean Sea, and finally ended up in Izmir. At the market in Izmir I saw my first eggplant: they were unbelievably beautiful, shiny and black. We went to a little bar in the market where they squeezed fresh fruit juices into gilded tea glasses: tangerine, lemon, apple, pomegranate, peach. I've always wanted to re-create that little juice bar in a farmers' market here. I also started drinking the very strong black Turkish coffee, poured into tiny porcelain cups. I still have one of those long-handled copper Turkish coffee-pots in my kitchen.

We finally said goodbye to Pierre and Richard in Izmir; they continued up to Istanbul, and Judy and I got rid of the Mini Cooper and took the ferry to Greece.

OCTOBER 2, 1969

*Dear Mother, Dad, Ellen, Bob, and little David—*

*I am writing to you from my bed in a very cheap taverna near the Acropolis in Athens. . . . I have really ambivalent feelings about Greece—about being here. I know I like it already. I love the little back streets and white squares, houses with shutters and bright blue morning glories hanging down from the rooftops. There are restaurants with tables outside that serve delicious seafood. Tonight I had octopus in wine sauce and last night charcoal broiled squid. The fish is accompanied with a salad of tomatoes, green peppers, onions, feta cheese and then garnished with Greek olives and sprinkled with wild marjoram. Yum . . .*

*Yes, I feel rather embarrassed about visiting here, which in most people's minds is condoning the fascist regime. . . . But I have so little money to spend, and such great interest in visiting the islands that I nearly rationalized it all away—my guilt, that is. . . .*

*Mother, the yoga sounds great. Judy practices whenever possible. And Dad—are you doing yoga too? And if not, why not?*

*I miss you all a whole lot, including Laura and Sue.*
*Love, Alice*

I did love Greece, it was true. Judy and I made our way to Corfu and pitched our tent on the beach right across from Albania, near the property of our Montessori teacher friend. Every day we would wake up with the sun rising over Albania, and in the afternoon we'd walk over to the other side of the island to watch the sun set. On our way back from watching the sunset, we always looked into the tavernas to see what they were cooking—and to see if there were any interesting-looking men. There were fires all over the island, from one side of the mountain to the other. You'd walk up close to the fire, watch the pigs turning on spits, and decide which pig looked the most worthy of eating, and where the best dancing would be happening that night.

*The place I feel most comfortable cooking now is over the fire—I've always had a fascination with it. In the mid-1970s my friend Natalie Waag and I went on a pilgrimage to visit the food writer Richard Olney at his home in Provence, and what struck me the most was how his fireplace was the centerpiece of his house. I thought it was a dream fireplace: made out of great river stones, with copper pots and cast iron pans hung in front, marble mortars and pestles on the mantel, and grills in the hearth. He was an intellectual but earthy cook who understood French cooking and complex sauces and processes. He had the knowledge and experience to refine dishes into a very simple, perfect, rustic cuisine. His cooking was direct but had a deep sophistication. That was one of the first times I saw someone cooking inside their house over their fireplace. He just sat there cooking wild chanterelles on the grill. It was like,* Why have a stove? *Truly.*

*Around then I also met Lulu Peyraud for the first time—the proprietress of Domaine Tempier winery in the South of France in Bandol, who became a mentor and muse of mine. Lulu too loved to cook by the fire more than anywhere else, grilling sardines in grape leaves or a leg of lamb on a spit. Her wine estate was built in the eighteenth century, when fireplaces were the only means of cooking. Her ancient Provençal fireplace was the length of a whole wall, at waist height, with a spit and a grill and places for big and small pots. Years later I modeled my own kitchen fireplace in the spirit of it.*

*Lulu is a complete natural on the grill. She made a ritual of cooking on the fire first thing in the morning. Watching her, I'd think,* Every day I want to start a fire in the fireplace when I wake up. *When my daughter was growing up, I did that a lot, and she'd wake up to the smell of the fire. She'd think,* Ah, someone's roasting peppers! *And it would get her out of bed and bring her downstairs— especially when she was a teenager and didn't want to get up!*

*The smell of a wood fire awakens people's senses—I've used that many, many times at Chez Panisse. At first we didn't have an open fire in the kitchen, though we did a lot of spontaneous cooking over fires in the backyard, much to the fire department's chagrin. About four or five years in, we built a cooking fireplace in the kitchen, and it really changed our cooking. That was when I was the main chef, and I always wanted to grill. Jean-Pierre Moullé was the saucier* and organized everything else—and while Jean-Pierre did have a passion for the grill, it was the job I always wanted. And I always, always built the fire.

With the grill, you learn by doing it over and over again, and it becomes second nature, like making bread: you just do it and do it and do it and do it—pretty soon you can just press on the skin and say, Ah, that's done. I'm always manipulating the fire under the meat—I know when certain parts of the meat are thicker than others, so I'm moving both the meat and the fire underneath. You learn how long it takes for a loin of pork to grill, for instance. I figured out it would take about half an hour and would need to rest for ten minutes, but there were all these variables in between. One of the great things we learned at Chez Panisse was if we put the grill on a slight angle, the fat from a duck breast would drip down the grill to a pan in front; that way we could have the duck breast over the fire, where it crisps the skin like a dream, but without the duck fat causing the coals to flare up.

So grilling is really about trial and error—you're testing all along the way. You're opening up the fish and putting it back on if it's not cooked. Or you're noticing that the part in the back along the bone is thicker—sometimes I'll prop a fish up against a log so that thicker piece gets cooked properly. I like that with grilling, you have room for correcting as you go along. And it offers so many different possibilities—making fish stock over the fire, for example, gives the soup a particular aroma. Spit-roasting a chicken over a fire is also a beautiful thing. It's endless, the ways we've used that fireplace.

After a few weeks on Corfu, Judy and I were thinking we wanted to stay in Greece for the rest of our lives. One day toward the end of our trip, we were walking through a little whitewashed town, and on one door we saw a FOR SALE sign. We knocked and discovered an inner courtyard filled with bleating sheep. We asked how much the whole house cost—four wings around a central courtyard—and it was $17,000. I thought, *Oh my God. Maybe I could get a bunch of friends together and figure out a way to buy this!* It was so incredibly beautiful. But I didn't buy it. (Why *didn't* I? I wish I had!)

After that I came back to Berkeley; David and I had broken up, and I had my own apartment for the first time in years. I painted it all white inside, and the doors cerulean blue, to be like Greece.

# CHAPTER 10

# Food and Film

I started working in earnest at the Montessori school in Berkeley—I was teaching pre-K, three- to six-year-olds. I was so nervous—all these little kids were running around, and you had to fling yourself down onto the ground with them, or else they simply didn't connect with you. I found I could engage them when we talked about food, or when I was reading a book like *Green Eggs and Ham*. That's where I excelled. One four-year-old made me read it over and over and over again, and every time I finished, I'd be egged on—green-egged on—to read it one more time. I knew it by heart and would act it out like a passionate melodrama; they were entranced.

I thought I could handle having my own class, but I couldn't. I'd never been with young children and didn't know their habits, or how to be with them. The training in England wasn't about getting comfortable with kids. I knew all the games but had never actually been around small children. One little kid in my class bit the other children all the

Berkeley Montessori School, circa 1969.

time. I kept grabbing him and saying, "Stop! You can't *do* this!" and getting more and more frustrated. But he kept biting the hell out of them until eventually, one time, I just bit him myself—to show him how it felt. It was a spur-of-the-moment, instinctual thing. I used to bite Ellen when we were wrestling and having a fight—she was so much bigger than me, and I'd get so angry that I couldn't do anything *but* bite her. But, of course, after I bit this boy, he started crying, and instantly I was unbelievably ashamed. I was working in tandem with another teacher in the class, and he was shocked.

I probably should have been fired, and eventually I was—but for wearing a see-through blouse. Bras had gone out with the Free Speech Movement, and we all wore diaphanous Hungarian blouses with flowers embroidered on the front. I got them at the flea market and wore them all the time with my blue jeans and sandals.

One day I was called into the office, and the administrators said, "Some of the parents have been complaining. Will you stop wearing those blouses?"

It took me by surprise. I didn't have any self-consciousness about those clothes—it was simply how young people were dressing then. For people to make an issue of it felt repressive, conservative—and especially strange in a Montessori environment. So I refused. And so they said, "Well, goodbye." It was a great moment for me, because I thought, *I don't want to work at a place where I'm not supported.* I was very aware of that and understood it—and wasn't deeply disappointed or crushed: *They don't want me here, so I don't want to be here.* I left feeling empowered in some way. Years later, when I occasionally had to fire someone at Chez Panisse, I thought a lot about those feelings—a firing is a two-way street. The person being fired should be helped to understand that they don't *want* to be in a place where they're not valued. You need to be in a place where you're cared about, and where you care about being.

I had also been discovering for some time that I wasn't a good teacher. I loved the Montessori philosophy and was glad to have the certificate. I thought it was absolutely worthwhile. But in practical terms, I didn't have what it took to teach young children. The realization had been dawning on me that I just wasn't patient and settled enough to do it.

Besides, I'd never thought teaching would be a lifelong choice for me. I got my Montessori certification because it seemed like a sensible idea, because I could earn more money and I was interested in the philosophy. But I didn't believe in the idea of a career—that word felt like a closing of doors. I hated the concept that you were going to get such-and-such a job, and progress and progress in it, and get a little higher status and a little more money, until before you knew it, there was your whole life. That sounded more like a life sentence to me—like forcing a straitjacket on. I was living in the moment and always felt like anything could happen.

And, of course, I knew you couldn't bite your students. You never hurt a child. Ever. It's very serious. There are so many ways to influence and teach children, but never with an action like that. I hadn't really digested the basic Montessori principle that you never discipline a child directly. It's about winning a child over to better behavior—creating another activity that's so irresistible that they're drawn to it. It's about empathy and awareness and empowerment. And I'm thinking about that in all the work I do now.

I have enormous respect for teachers because of that part of my life. I completely empathize with them and know that teaching is so challenging. I think a lot about the fact that I was teaching only *really* little children, and I still felt that I didn't have enough to give them—truly, I didn't *know* enough to teach a three-year-old. I couldn't begin to answer their questions: "Why does the cat die?" "Why can't we go outside now?" They would ask me such simple, profound questions that by the end of every day, I felt I didn't have even a three-year-old's education.

*A lot of the chefs at Chez Panisse have been incredible teachers, too— like Lindsey, who eventually did start the restaurant with me and was our pastry chef for years and years. Would that I could be non-judgmental enough to be a really good teacher, like Lindsey. I aspire to that, but I fall short. I'm not patient enough to be a teacher—and that's an understatement! That's why I have such admiration for them. They're the most valuable people, and we need to train more of them.*

Some of the greatest teachers in my life have been people I'm passionately in love with and admire. When I was in love with David, I learned about art and printing and books. His passion was so contagious, I absorbed it easily—it was really like I had been spoon-fed. Many of the men I've fallen in love with first became fascinating to me because of the work that they did. How they looked was sort of secondary—I've always been attracted to a physically diverse group of people. I see their particular passion first.

While I was teaching Montessori, I saw a lot of Martine and Claude, who were still living in their old Victorian house.

Patrick Straram, a poet, writer, and film critic from Quebec, lived with them for a while. Patrick's friends called him "the Bison Ravi," the Ecstatic Buffalo, and he was crazy in all ways, drunk, out there, but also fascinating and smart. He came to stay with Martine and Claude for two days but ended up staying for a whole year. He used to sit out on the steps in front of their house and eat oysters out of a can for breakfast.

Patrick was friends with Tom Luddy, who ran the Telegraph Repertory Theater, an art house cinema that screened Buster Keaton revivals, the new Andy Warhol films, French New Wave, and political documentaries. Tom Luddy had run several film societies at Cal and was deeply involved in the Free Speech Movement, too, showing all kinds of films about the protests. Apparently he had been at UC Berkeley at the same time as me, though I didn't know him then; he'd been a senior when I was a sophomore. Patrick, the Bison Ravi, introduced Tom Luddy and Martine to each other, and then Martine thought I should go out with Tom.

One of my very first impressions of Tom was of his hat—he always wore a straight-brimmed black felt hat that had a bit of a cowboy feel to it, often with a black leather jacket and jeans. That was his uniform of the time—like James Dean in *Rebel Without a Cause* meets *The Magnificent Seven*.

When I fell in love with Tom, I absorbed his passion for film—thanks to him, film became the second great passion of my life. Sometimes we would watch three 16 mm films a day—we're talking a big old projector that he would have to set up every time. We'd watch experimental films of Bruce Connor, Max Ophuls's *The Earrings of Madame de . . .* and *Letter from an Unknown Woman*, Kenneth Anger's *Scorpio Rising,* Fellini's *La Strada*, and Alain Resnais's *Last Year at Marienbad* and *Hiroshima Mon Amour*. He'd get all these films because he was screening them for the Telegraph Repertory Theater; sometimes he'd screen a film for a group, sometimes it was just the two of us at his home. Under Tom's bed were reels of Godard's *A Woman Is a Woman* stacked up. Treasures.

So I was cooking for Tom, things like chicken with garlic or baked fish and a *tarte au citron*, and he was showing me movies. He liked everything I cooked; he was a fantastic eater. He would always say, "This is just *great*, Alice. This is just great." He thought I made the best food on the planet. I'd cook while he was setting up the projector and screen, and we'd eat dinner and drink wine, then pull the shades down and watch the movie. We lived together in his little bungalow in Berkeley on the border of Oakland; I had barely had time to settle into my whitewashed apartment before I moved in with Tom. (I wasn't so much nomadic as a serial monogamist.) Tom would try to find films he thought I'd love—and still does. (He knew that if a film got too "difficult," I'd leave the room.) Even today he'll come around to my house and put a little stack of movies on my front porch.

Tom knew people in all dimensions: he was friends with poets, composers, filmmakers, novelists, intellectuals, and musicians. His curiosity was expansive, endless. He was like an enzyme, forever making connections between his friends, bringing people together, making reactions happen, then getting out of the way. It was selfless—he never did it for his personal gain, just for the joy of watching new relationships form. He could have fascinating visions: he might seat the

*Interplayers' Tom Luddy: No camp please.*

Tom Luddy, circa 1969.

Czech film director Miloš Forman next to Shirley MacLaine and see what could happen. And something generally did. Those visions could be interdisciplinary—he could match up musicians with street activists—and they could be political or cultural or both.

Tom's father had been a longtime chairman of the Democratic Party in Westchester County, who worked for both John F. and Robert Kennedy, so Tom had grown up absorbing progressive political engagement from him. I had the impression that his mother came from a vaguely literary background—she had corresponded with the great Irish playwright Sean O'Casey. Tom's older brother had died when Tom was six years old, and I think Tom's mother never recovered from that grief. Tom was then the oldest, and I suspect he felt that responsibility from an early age.

It wasn't until Catholic high school, in White Plains, New York, that film became a passion for him. Several progressive, radical priests there had a big impact on him; apparently he had a seminal moment with an incredible teacher, Father Bert Marino, who once told the religion class, "The spiritual crises of our time are better explored in these new movies coming out than anywhere else. If any of you want to know what I'm talking about, I'd be glad to take us on a field trip to a theater in Manhattan, where I just saw Antonioni's *L'Avventura* and Bergman's *Through a Glass Darkly*." (Of course, some student piped up to say, "But Father, those films are

on the condemned list for the Catholic Legion of Decency!")
Thanks to this teacher, Tom got turned on to Antonioni,
Bergman, Fellini, and Resnais, and by the time he arrived in
Berkeley in 1961, he was deeply in love with film—and the
profound effect it could have on people, politics, and culture.

Tom has a photographic memory—once he sees something, he has it forever. He knew my childhood friends'
phone numbers by heart just by glancing at them once, and
he still knows them today. That photographic memory is
part of why he was so extraordinary at connecting people
who were going to like each other. He was a matchmaker in
every possible way—in art, work, love—and maybe most of
all, in terms of simply helping people. I didn't know I was
learning about how to make those sorts of connections
from Tom—I thought I was just learning about film!—but
as we were together, I got some of that through osmosis.
Up until that time, I had been much more self-absorbed.
But Tom showed me how much happiness you can get out
of bringing a diverse group of people together and starting
conversations—and what good can come from it.

*Because of Tom, directors would often come through Berkeley to
show their films at Telegraph Rep or, later, the Pacific Film Archive, which Tom founded in 1972. Tom and I shared a house on
Dana Street that was very little—small kitchen, small living
room. But we had two bedrooms: one on the main floor, and a tiny*

*room upstairs where the filmmakers would sleep when they came to town. Tom was always inviting film people to come stay with us. After a director's film screened, he would bring him or her over to our house for dinner—or, after the restaurant opened, to Chez Panisse. Thanks to Tom, a lot of incredible directors I've been in awe of have come through the restaurant: Werner Herzog, Roberto Rossellini, Wim Wenders, Ang Lee, Godfrey Reggio, Errol Morris, Dušan Makavejev, Ousmane Sembène, Howard Hawks, and Andrei Konchalovsky.*

*Once when Glauber Rocha, a radical filmmaker from Brazil, came to Berkeley, he stayed with us in our little house on Dana Street. Rocha was out there, really out there, with uncombed hair and wild eyes. I vividly remember his film* Black God, White Devil; *it starts with an airplane coming in for a landing in Rio, then cuts to a golf course and somebody teeing off, then cuts right to the favelas. It was such a clear, visceral example of the savage inequalities of life around this globe. It was an incredibly graphic film, showing Brazil's ghettos and golf courses side by side—and what's so shocking is that this disparity still exists now and may even be worse.*

*Tom once invited Francis Ford Coppola and George Lucas to meet Akira Kurosawa at a dinner at Chez Panisse. It was another one of his inspired visions—Tom thought it would be a great place for the four of them to discuss the production of the 1980 film* Kagemusha—*and I loved having the restaurant be an element in his master plan. I loved helping Tom make these connections happen, doing my part by inviting all these creative, brilliant people* to dinner. And it made Chez Panisse into the kind of place where I wanted to be. (I'm afraid that all I really remember of the Kurosawa evening was that Kurosawa wore an all-white linen suit and was quite tall.)

I was always so concerned about making these people from around the world feel comfortable and at home in the restaurant. When Andrei Konchalovsky came to Chez Panisse, he asked for a vodka. I was so embarrassed we didn't have it that I ran out, jumped in my car, drove to the liquor store, raced back—and went through a red light a block or two from Chez Panisse and was pulled over. The policemen asked, "Have you been drinking?" I said, "Absolutely not." They said, "Can you walk in a line?" They detained me for fifteen minutes at least, and I was beside myself. Fortunately the vodka bottles were hidden under the seat of the car.

Tom once brought in the legendary Indian director Satyajit Ray, too, though I'm embarrassed to say I hadn't seen his films at that point. It's particularly a shame because I would have loved talking to him about his Apu trilogy, which I saw later; Tom took me to see those three films at the Telegraph Rep, and I learned a whole lot from them. There's an old woman in the first film who beautifully symbolizes the wisdom of old age and the place for that in a family. The grandmother knew how to navigate between households, moving from one house to another before she wore out her welcome. And even though she was skin and bones and bent over double, she had the greatest disposition. She must have been in her nineties, but she was a real force in the family and was bonded intimately with all the young girls. I love that about those Satyajit Ray films—you see *the grandmother, the mother, and the child all sleeping in the same bed, people of all ages connected together.*

*Film directors were always a little bit distracted at the restaurant. A lot of those guys didn't really eat, they were there to socialize: drinking, arriving late or early, ordering things that weren't on the menu. It was like herding cats. Not that I objected! It was more that I felt bad intruding on these heady meetings of theirs. You'd have to interrupt some big, deep conversation to say, "Excuse me, what would you like to eat?" They were in their own minds—I always just wanted to say, "The dinner's on me, and here it is." But they were directors, they also wanted to direct! The one director Tom brought who was the most interested in food was Roberto Rossellini: we seated their big party in our private room. (Sadly, it doesn't exist anymore—we called it the* cabinet particulier, *and it had a table that seated six to eight people.) Rossellini was so interested in food—he ordered the food and wine for the whole table, and was so present. I didn't need to worry about him at all.*

My experience of movies before Tom was slim. I didn't have many moviegoing experiences as a child; I was very scared by one of the first I saw, *The Wizard of Oz*. The witch, the monkeys, the music—all of it!—frightened me. But I started to get into films shortly before Tom. Jon Cott and I saw the *Gorky* trilogy at a theater in Hampstead that winter we were there, and I was so moved by the film. It was in three parts, *The Childhood of Maxim Gorky*, *My Apprenticeship*, and *My Universities*, and we went on three different days to see it—

it was an epic experience. And it was imprinted on me in some indelible way, as if it were stamped on my forehead. It was snowing outside the theater in Hampstead, and the movie was like hell in Russia, a bleak vision in the snow. I felt how powerful—and how sensual—film could be.

Early in our relationship, Tom showed me another incredible Soviet film. *Shadows of Forgotten Ancestors*, by the Armenian director Sergei Parajanov, was a love story about poor farmers in the mountains of the Ukraine. The film was *so* passionate—talk about passion! I don't want to give the plot away, but the beauty and authenticity of the story were so striking, set against snowy mountains in winter and green hillsides in spring. Throughout the movie, the characters wear the most beautiful traditional Ukrainian clothing: skins and furs and hats and scarves and red coats, surrounded by the smoke of Orthodox churches. I watched it and I thought, *Whoa! I want to go live in Russia!* Tom was a Russophile—he read everything of Chekhov, Tolstoy, Gogol, the whole gang. He was absorbed in every part of the culture, from dance to music to literature to film, and it felt transgressive at the time because we were still in the middle of the Cold War.

Tom was something of an underground diplomat, vis-à-vis filmmakers. We would go to Bali's, a place in the city that had great Armenian food. The owner was Armen Baliantz (she was the mother of Jeannette Etheredge, who later owned and ran Tosca's, the historic North Beach café and bar), and everybody called her Madame Bali. She made

Bali's into a salon for bohemian artists, politicians, and defectors from the Soviet Union like the ballet dancer Rudolf Nureyev. We used to go there for their rack of lamb with pomegranate glaze, and lots of vodka.

*In 1987 I was invited on a "gastronomic tour" of the Soviet Union with a group of food writers and cooks like Paula Wolfert, Patty Unterman, Bill Rice, Joan Nathan, and several others. Because of those Russian films I'd seen, I'd always wanted to go there, so when I finally got a chance, I jumped at it. First we visited the Baltic States. We left Estonia for Lithuania the day before Estonia, Lithuania, and Latvia revolted against the Soviet Union. We'd thought we were going on a tour with a Lithuanian gastronome, this woman who had sold the trip to the government as a culinary tour of the Soviet Union. But unknown to us, she was really in the Lithuanian underground and was using this trip so she could be part of fomenting the revolution!*

*So as soon as we landed in Lithuania, our guide abandoned us to a group of Lithuanians who were teaching at a cooking school in a tiny little village, and we felt like we had gone a hundred years back in time. It was nothing like the films I had seen—not beautiful in that way. It was completely isolated. We were supposed to be sampling and tasting the food of students who were learning to cook, and as we watched them present their dishes, we were thinking,* What is this? *It was incomprehensible, usually with lots of potatoes, but we had to be really, really nice. One day they spit-roasted a cake! The table was always set so elaborately, with napkins twisted into little tortured knots and stuck into the wineglasses, and so much silverware on either side of the plate. It was the Lithuanian idea of haute cuisine, I think.*

*Eventually our supposed guide did come back and rescue us, and we continued the tour. We were drinking so much hard liquor and vodka with every meal that it's a miracle I can remember anything from the trip. There was so, so much hard liquor. They would put a big bottle of vodka on the table and refill our glasses endlessly, and we all felt it would be uncivil not to drink what they'd poured. One time in Latvia, Paula and Patty literally had to carry me out of a bus because I was so drunk. They had to carry me up the stairs, one holding my legs and the other my head and shoulders, and drop me in bed. I've never been so drunk in my life.*

*There was no produce in Moscow. The only person with salads and vegetables at the market had come over from Georgia, more than a thousand miles away. I felt really sorry for Muscovites— there really was nothing there. And there were no restaurants in any of the places we visited, so we usually had to eat in our hotels. The hotel food was just basic and forgettable, like bland, steam-table cafeteria food—no blinis and caviar.*

*The only place where we got into the region's gastronomy was Georgia. We had idyllic days there. When I got off the plane, a Georgian woman greeted us and welcomed us to the country. I was so charmed by her that I said, "You know, I could live here." I had a gut feeling from the moment we landed, I don't know where it came from. I stepped onto the ground, and it was something about the air, the light, the atmosphere—suddenly we were in the Mediterranean, a world away from Moscow. It was like,* Oh my God, I'm home.

*We went into Tbilisi, and the cabdriver who drove us into town wouldn't let us pay. Our hotel had a dining room and a great big table set for us, and each place setting had a full bottle of champagne, white wine, red wine, sweet wine, and a hard liquor—five full bottles in a little arc around each plate! Tom had warned me about this; he knew filmmakers from that area and had often gone to big filmmaker banquets when he visited. He said it was the only time he's ever taken his drink and quietly poured it into a houseplant, like in those old silent movies. We all felt that way. There was just too much to drink—you had to toast over and over and over. None of us could find a potted plant.*

*The landscape was beautiful in Georgia: very Mediterranean, with olive trees. We went to the farmers' market, and I said, "This is the kind of farmers' market I want to have in San Francisco." All the local farmers were there, each with his or her own small table, and it looked like they had all brought the beautiful fruits and vegetables they had grown in their backyards. One farmer had a sack of flour he had hand-ground himself, and if you wanted some, he'd put a scoop of flour onto a piece of paper and tie it up into a little bundle for you. And twenty beautiful men with black handlebar mustaches were selling pomegranates, hawking them in the most seductive ways, breaking them apart, offering them to us. Twenty different people were selling lettuce, but each had his own clients. It seemed so egalitarian—the city felt neither too rich nor too poor, just prosperous enough, and everyone participated in this market that was so exactly about what was grown there. One night in Tbilisi, we went to see a Georgian dance. The women glided around in long black dresses as if they were skating, and the men were wearing red coats and doing backflips. It was so beautiful, so romantic. I've always wanted to go back. That was just like the films I'd seen.*

I saw films from all over the world with Tom. We saw lots of Godard, just when they were coming out in theaters—and Truffaut, all those French New Wave guys. I definitely responded to these films in part because they were French, and

Cinephiles at an early Telluride Film Festival (from left): Barbet Schroeder, Manny Farber, Tom Luddy, Ed Lachman, Patricia Patterson, Werner Herzog, Jean-Pierre Gorin, and Brooks Riley.

I was such a Francophile, and Tom would tell me all about the actors and the directors. Martine and Claude would come over and watch movies with us, and they loved them. Once Godard actually showed up at our house for dinner when he was in town, and Jean-Pierre Gorin, Godard's co-director at the time, came, too.

Godard was very intimidating. He wasn't into food for sure—or talking. Or at least, he wasn't into talking to me! Every time we were left alone together, he said absolutely nothing, as if I didn't exist. I was mostly in the kitchen that night preparing a special dinner for him, a classic quiche Lorraine, a green salad, and my signature chocolate mousse *au Grand Marnier*. Claude and Martine were there, too. Claude remembers we served Godard a fancy wine, a delicious Bordeaux, and he took this beautiful, perfect red and poured a glass of water into it. Everyone was shocked. Godard was the sort of person who had no problem drinking instant coffee from a vending machine. It surprised me that someone so brilliant and artistic didn't care about food.

His co-director Jean-Pierre Gorin was intimidating, too—he was a real intellectual, a profound writer who was always interested in engaging you in a political or philosophical conversation. But at least *he* talked to me. And he talked to me about food, and we connected about that. His sensuality and flirtatiousness and wicked sense of humor really appealed to me, and he was handsome, too, like a

French movie star—dark hair, dark eyes, very rugged. I always fantasized that Tom and Jean-Pierre and I were like the two guys and the woman in Truffaut's *Jules et Jim*.

One time Jean-Pierre wanted to cook a meal for Tom and me and some of our friends, and he was making a rabbit at our house. (I remember it as a fish, but Jean-Pierre assures me it was rabbit.) His preparations took all afternoon, because the rabbit was a beast: a "true American specimen," as Jean-Pierre described it, that was "about the size of a kangaroo and as tough as one too." He fought valiantly with it, but in the end he took the rabbit out of the oven, tasted it, didn't like it—then went outside and threw it in the garbage can! That's how much he cared. And then, of course, *I* had to cook dinner.

*In the years that followed, Jean-Pierre started spending more and more time in California, and became close with Tom's whole film crowd. In fact, when* Apocalypse Now *was being made in 1976, Francis Ford Coppola sent a telegram to Jean-Pierre, inviting him to fly out to help with the making of the film for a few months; if he joined them in the Philippines, Francis wrote, Jean-Pierre could teach him about Godard and in return Francis would teach him about making big Hollywood films. (Needless to say, Jean-Pierre agreed to go join Francis's army.) Shortly after Jean-Pierre returned from his* Apocalypse Now *endeavor, I ended up marrying him so he could get his green card; Jean-Pierre was interested in working with the film critic Manny Farber in San Diego, and wanted to stay in the United States permanently. Tom always knew I had a thing for Jean-Pierre; by that time Tom and I had split up, and Tom was in love with his future wife, Monique, so the green card marriage was probably Tom's clever idea.*

*I admit I totally got into it. I have a picture of myself in my wedding dress, coming out the door of my house on the way to city hall. I was dressed as a Gypsy, with this incredible pink silk scarf tied to my head, a 1920s-style rosette on the side, a long pink dress, and a red Japanese kimono. Jean-Pierre and I went to Oakland City Hall with Tom and my friend Sharon as our witnesses. Tom and Monique were renting a house up in the hills of Berkeley, and they threw us a big party afterward, with lots of dancing and wine and food. There had been a deep ongoing flirtation between Jean-Pierre and me, or at least I thought so, and I was crazy about him—but he wasn't crazy about me. I remember going up with him to the bedroom in Tom's house that night and thinking, Ah! Finally we can consummate this! And Jean-Pierre said, no go. I had always wanted to marry a Frenchman, and I imagined he had always wanted to marry a cook. But it was platonic all the way. I was disappointed but not hurt—we never really lived together, and we ended the "marriage" about seven years later when he was interested in another woman. We've remained friends all these years.*

Around then I met Les Blank, too—he was a local filmmaker I'd heard about and yet another friend of Tom's.

What attracted me to Les was that he was endlessly curious and questioning and always wanted to know about food in a deep way.

Les was from the South—at least, he had a southern drawl, so I always assumed he was a southerner. He had parties in Berkeley in his backyard and a lot of girlfriends. He was strong and silent and always there with the camera, of course. I went to the Jazz Festival in New Orleans with him

one time, when it was really hot. We went to this little restaurant in New Orleans that was having a crawfish boil. They put newspaper down all over our table, boiled the crawfish they'd just caught, drained them, and dumped the whole pot right out onto the table. I thought it was so amazing to have that big pile of crawfish: shelling them with our hands, dipping them in this spicy sauce, and eating them like that. Then Les took me in a rowboat up the bayou to visit his musician friends. We went to a dinner at a little place right on the water—Spanish moss, cypresses, the whole bayou vision. It had a hand-painted sign out front that read GOO, CAT AND GAR—those were the three fish they had. And so that's what we had! At one point when we were going through the swamps out there by the GOO, CAT AND GAR cottage, Les rowing the boat, it got stuck on a cypress knee. Les jumped into the bayou and swam out in front, pulling the boat along! He wasn't afraid of the alligators in the water at all—he was a great swimmer and athlete.

*In 1976 Les filmed the first garlic festival at Chez Panisse—at Tom's prompting, I think. From what Les documented, he made a terrific film called* Garlic Is as Good as Ten Mothers—*I've always loved that Chinese proverb. Nicholas Ray, the director of* Rebel Without a Cause, *was at that first festival, too: he wore a red shirt, sat at a big long table, and was having a great time. He's in Les's film. You have to look carefully to spot him, but he's in there.*

As I've said, back when I was writing those "Alice's Restau-rant" columns with David, I began thinking maybe I should start a restaurant instead of always having so many people over to my house and cooking for them. Tom picked up on that feeling, too. He could see what my passion really was, and after Montessori was out, I was a little adrift. He was in-strumental in encouraging me to think about it in a real and serious way. He heard me say, "I want to open a restaurant," and he said, "Yes, you *should* do it. Let's go out and see what other restaurants are like!" He was my biggest cheerleader.

So as I was plotting to open this restaurant, mulling it over in my mind, Tom and I did a lot of eating out so I could see how other places were run. He was always up on the lat-est little restaurants—he liked that scene. Some of the spots we went to were great; others, less so. A French place on South Van Ness in San Francisco served up a whole roasted duck with a tinfoil covering in the shape of a duck on top. That duck-shaped tinfoil was in high demand: if two parties in the restaurant ordered duck at the same time, one table had to wait until the tinfoil cover came off and could be re-used. And if three people ordered duck at the same time—disaster. At another restaurant, we leaned against a curtain, and the curtain rod came down on our heads.

We went to so many places, to Vanessi's and Tommaso's, two popular old North Beach Italian restaurants, to Tosca's for cocktails, and to La Bourgogne. Some were quite fancy, like La Bourgogne—I always had to save up my money for that one. La Bourgogne's soufflé Grand Marnier, with crème anglaise poured around it, was the most exquisite thing—it impressed me and convinced me I'd have to have soufflés at the restaurant I was starting. The waiter would come out to the table with the soufflé all puffed up, take a perfect scoop of it, gently put it onto my plate, and pour the crème anglaise onto it. It was heaven.

Some of the restaurants we went to weren't fancy at all. At Yuet Lee in Chinatown, we ordered salt and pepper squid—and at Tommaso's, I loved the pizzas with garlic. I absolutely fell for that, and those were probably the first times I truly noticed and appreciated garlic. There was some sort of convergence of taste for me—the garlic flavor was associated with that taste of *really* good food from the wood oven.

*As you know by now, garlic became a huge obsession at Chez Panisse after we started doing an annual Bastille Day garlic festival in 1976. We used a lot more garlic at the restaurant after that. More than anything, it was about awareness. We learned that you couldn't chop all your garlic for the whole night ahead of time—you had to chop it as you went along, so it wouldn't oxidize. And the stronger the garlic got, the longer you had to cook it—usually it was at its strongest around Christmas, January, and February. You had to take out the little green sprout in the middle of each clove, because that could be bitter. And we learned that garlic is spoiled when it's burned or browned in any way. I can tell right away when I go into a restaurant with bad garlic.*

*We learned, too, that there is more to garlic than the papery white heads; when the garlic is growing and you thin a row so that the heads can mature and grow to full size, the young green garlic shoots you pull up are delicious, too. We experimented with a soup in the springtime made from that green garlic, from what had been thinned. I loved the taste of that soup—it was so pure, a really gentle flavor. We'd make it with potatoes and even stewed some of the green tops for garnish. You always want garlic to taste like that. It's so rare, though. I think we invented that soup on our own—I don't remember getting a recipe for it, although various recipes existed out there. I just know we responded to that unique taste. We made that soup for James Beard the first time he came to the restaurant. It was in the early days, and we'd referred to it on the menu as young garlic. James said, very emphatically, "You don't call it young garlic—it's green garlic!" He knew all about it.*

None of these restaurants were like what I cooked at home, and none looked the way I imagined mine would. I was taking notes in my head about restaurants, compiling a database: how the waiters dressed and how they treated their customers, the brightness of the lights, the color of the paint on the walls. It was about a lot more than the food—I wanted to figure out the running of the business. At the time I thought the perfect size would be forty seats, with a bar at the end of the room, like the little family-owned places in France. I wanted mirrors on the walls and golden lighting like at Martine's house; and I wanted checkered tablecloths and real linen napkins and little pigeonholes where the regulars' napkins could go, like in Paris.

Gibson House in Bolinas was my favorite restaurant. It was in an old Victorian house covered with orange and yellow nasturtiums—I loved that. The owner was a woman who had old vintage patchwork quilts hanging from the walls, which, of course, interested Martine and me. And they did a duck *à l'orange* dish that was served with the same nasturtiums on the plate. I thought, *What is this?* It was the first time I'd seen an edible flower on a plate. And no tinfoil, thank God.

Gibson House, Bolinas, California.

We went up to Bolinas a lot back then, Claude and Martine and Tom and I—we'd take that drive in our little old red Comet on a Sunday, following Highway 1 along the coast or Sir Francis Drake Boulevard, until we got to the Bolinas Lagoon and the unmarked turnoff for the town. Tom knew some poets who lived in Bolinas, a group from the New York School of Poetry who had decamped to the West Coast: Ted Berrigan, Joanne Kyger, Bill Berkson, and Tom Clark. Tom did his usual stuff, bringing up books that people needed to read and screening films. Bolinas was a radical little community and a real cultural scene, with writers and intellectuals who had escaped the city and gone back to the land. We'd pick blackberries in Bolinas, find watercress in the streams—it was really early foraging. Picking the berries was prompted by Martine; she would notice them out the window and spur us to go out and gather them, and then she'd make blackberry jam.

*After that I didn't go back to Bolinas for easily twenty-five years—I was too busy with the restaurant. But in the mid-1990s, when my friend Susie invited me to her home there, I rediscovered it. I was so happy to find that much of what was in Bolinas in the 1960s was—is!—still there. Thank God for the incredible environmentalists back then in the 1960s who made the whole coastline around Bolinas into a series of national parks and watersheds—from the Marin headlands and Muir Woods up to Point Reyes National*

*Seashore. You're only forty-five minutes from San Francisco, and yet you're in wilderness. And Bolinas can never get more populated because officials said, "Only this many houses can be built here, no more." It had to do with water rights and protecting the water table. That preserved coastline is such a gift—they really were thinking of the future for our children. I find my solace now in Bolinas—it's a refuge for me. My friends Susie and Mark let me stay in their house every year. What a gift. I still pick the blackberries and make jam there with my daughter every August at her birthday.*

Tom took me to a house in the hills of Berkeley once, a sort of religious commune, where we were invited for dinner. All these gurus of the time were present, and Tom's previous girlfriend Diana had got involved with a New Age religion called the Foundation of Revelation. Diana was one of the eight wives of this guru Chiranjiva and looked the part: long blond hair, long peach robe. For dinner they served us whole overcooked carrots with the skin still on. I was appalled. It was so un-French. I thought, *Barbarians! Carrots with the skins on!* No question it was more nutritious, but carrots with the skins on! Tom and I both agreed it was a weird scene.

Around that time Tom took a trip to Paris to see his film-maker friends, and I tagged along because I wanted to expand my research by eating in restaurants there. We stopped over in New York briefly on our way to France; we were en route to Brooklyn for some reason, came out of the subway exit in the St. George Hotel—and basically walked right onto the set of the first *Godfather* movie! We ran into Francis Ford Coppola, who was more or less an unknown then— Tom had befriended him (of course) a couple years before, when Francis had come to San Francisco to start American Zoetrope with George Lucas, but I didn't know who he was. Francis was happy to see Tom and talked to us for a few minutes about how he thought he was going to get fired from this Italian mafia film he was directing. It wasn't until *The Godfather* came out in 1972 and became the classic that it is that I realized what we'd stumbled into.

*Tom later ended up working for Francis as a special projects producer, so I got to know Francis and his wife, Ellie, too. I was a little intimidated by him—he was a real director with a strong voice, often preoccupied and in his head a lot of the time. He liked to cook, though, and we bonded over that. But I felt really close to his wife, Ellie, right away—she came from an Irish background, like me, was about my size, and was easy to be with.*

*Francis had a big old Victorian house on Fillmore, with a whole movie theater downstairs and a swimming pool in the backyard. He would hold forth over pizzas or pasta. I learned how to drink tequila there with Jean-Pierre Gorin. He'd cut slices of lemon and cover them half in sugar, half in coffee grounds. You'd take a shot of tequila and then put the lemon in your mouth. You'd go to the moon before you even tasted anything.*

When we got to Paris, Tom and I went straight to the Cinémathèque Française, the massive, storied film archive that collects and preserves all films of note from around the world. The Cinémathèque Française was the incubator for the French New Wave—Godard and Truffaut educated themselves about film there in the 1950s, and the *cinémathèque* helped them become critics. We met Henri Langlois while we were there, the legendary character who had founded the *cinémathèque* and one of Tom's great heroes. The French government had fired Langlois in 1968, which, because cinema was so important to French culture, led to gigantic street protests in Paris until he was reinstated. Amazing films played all the time at the Cinémathèque Française, at every hour of the day or night—films by Renoir or Sergei Eisenstein or Luis Buñuel; I wanted to live right next door to it.

We stayed at Tom's friend's apartment, Pascal Aubier (yet another director); he lived at 1 Rue de Fleurus, right across the street from where Gertrude Stein had lived, near Luxembourg Gardens. We ate out at cheap little places in the Latin Quarter with Tom's film friends. There were a few gastronomes in the crew, but mostly we ate at regrettable places. One was a shock because it looked so charming on the outside, with pink curtains and tablecloths and a shelf with beautiful terrines all around, almost like Elizabeth David's shop—it had all the right touches. But the food just wasn't good: soggy *frites*, mussels that weren't fresh the way I remembered them on my college trip. We had terrible restaurant luck the whole time we were there. The food at one place was so terrifically bad that we stole a copper pot to get even (a little one).

But our food experiences weren't entirely awful. I took Tom to E. Dehillerin, the amazing old shop near the big Les Halles market that sold restaurant equipment. Sara and I had discovered it when we were there in 1965. That place really fed into my fantasy of a restaurant and a kitchen full of copper pots. It had everything: I marveled at all the special equipment and tools that I'd seen in the pages of *Larousse Gastronomique*. And while we were there, I ducked into Les Halles, too, a vibrant, busy, important place in the heart of Paris, where you would bump into purveyors and get in the way of carts of whole carcasses. Milk-fed calves hung on big hooks, giant fish rested on ice, and there were mounds and mounds of vegetables and cheeses. That market was the safety net for a lot of people in Paris, because the left-over food was given away at the end of every day. That was the last time I went to the original Les Halles; in 1971, the year we opened Chez Panisse, the old market was demolished and the food market was moved outside Paris, near the airport, giving priority to international purveyors. Because of that, the small organic farmers around Paris were marginalized.

We also went to Lionel Poilâne's bakery in Paris for the first time and had a loaf of levain bread there. Poilâne was famous by then; it was *the* bakery in Paris, on the Rue du Cherche-Midi. The levain looked fantastic—this big old crusty loaf—and the flavor was sublime, a very subtle sourdough that takes on the character of the yeast. Everything about it was unique, because Lionel had taken the traditional French bread and made it into something extraordinary. He'd perfected his own flour, his water, the sourdough, and the type of wood used in the oven, and all of it went into the flavor of the bread. I believe that in some ways, the good bread we have here in the United States now all came from that big beautiful levain loaf that Lionel made. I can't think of anyone who's making truly great bread without knowing about it.

Before we left, Tom and I went outside Paris to visit Agnès Varda and Jacques Demy. Agnès and Jacques were married, and both were directors—she of *Uncle Yanco*, and he of *The Umbrellas of Cherbourg*, with Catherine Deneuve. The two of them were in California a lot around then, in the mix of the American counterculture, I think because they were disappointed with the way the French underground culture had developed. Agnès had just made a short documentary about Huey Newton, the leader of the Black Panthers. At the time Jacques and Agnès were living on Noirmoutier-en-l'Île, an island just off the coast of Pays de la Loire. We stayed with them in the old windmill where they lived. One night Jacques Demy's mother came over and made us a *blanquette de veau*, a very classic French stew, with a little white wine from the Loire Valley and a light sauce. It was so tender—veal in France was a whole different thing. She used the little white onions from her garden, and served it with small new potatoes.

*Tom later started the Telluride Film Festival in 1972. His very good friends, Bill and Stella Pence, lived in Telluride and wanted to do something to help the town's economy. They all had a mutual love of film, so they decided to hold a film festival there over Labor Day weekend every year. Telluride is way up in the mountains of Colorado, and it was utterly charming from the first time I saw it: it was built in the 1870s and was a silver and gold mining camp, this very tiny town in a box canyon ringed all around by gigantic red rock mountains. In September, when the aspens are changing colors, the sky is so blue, the clouds are so white, and the wild chanterelles are sprouting up everywhere, it takes your breath away it's so stunning. (Telluride is now officially a Slow Food city—and has a fantastic farmers' market.)*

*At the beginning, Jean-Pierre Gorin and all of Tom's friends were there, and we all hung out at the Sheridan Bar in town. Tom knew how much I loved old films, so my job was to entertain the incredible older film stars who came: Viola Dana came, Gloria Swanson came, and one time the French film director Abel Gance came—he was ninety-four. The main street was empty of cars, and there was Abel Gance, with his big cowboy hat, ambling up and down the middle of the street. I was awestruck. They showed his classic split-screen 1927 silent film,* Napoléon, *in the outdoor the-*

*ater, and accompanied it with a live orchestra that played the score by Carmine Coppola, the father of Francis Ford Coppola. You felt like you were going back in time.*

*One year Tom had Russian and Chinese filmmakers come at the same time, and he set up a big debate between them in the park. Tom has never stopped bringing people together in a way where they appreciate each other and can build relationships. He taught me that people act differently with one another in the mountains of Colorado, surrounded by the splendor of nature and the camaraderie of young filmmakers.*

*I really love film festivals. I've always thought that maybe in my old age I'll just wander from one festival to another. (I'm counting on being able to see and hear!) It's a way I can just drop out—I get so absorbed in the films, they take me out of my life. And they inspire and educate me. Food and film are the two great passions of my life. Especially black-and-white films from the 1930s! I watch Turner Classic Movies every night—three films a day when I'm feeling really bad. If I didn't have Turner Classics, I don't know what would happen to me. Watching movies releases my energy, helps me to decompress—it's like therapy. You're just in them. I've got most of my information in life from movies—really, that's how I learn.*

Kermit Lynch emerging from Richard Olney's wine cellar.

# CHAPTER II

# **Terroir**

By 1970 I was spending all my time scouting around Berkeley, looking for spots for a restaurant. But I was looking mostly at commercial buildings—one was up on College and Alcatraz, and one was across the street from the Claremont Hotel, next to Jackson Liquors. None appealed—they had hardly any windows and no character. I was almost at the point of asking myself, *What am I doing?* But then I came across a spot behind a popular student hangout, Caffe Mediterraneum, on Telegraph Avenue right by campus; there was a little alleyway parallel to Telegraph and a small brick building in the back. When I came across the FOR RENT sign in the alleyway, I said, *Oh, yes. It's the crêperie.* I absolutely saw a small restaurant there: a modest little place that would serve traditional buckwheat crêpes and cider.

I knew how to make crêpes and loved doing it. There's a beautiful immediacy about them, like fresh tortillas or puris, where you're making them and serving them right away. You have that wonderful made-to-order experience. I imagined it spilling out onto the alleyway, a handful of outdoor tables with all my friends gathering around and ordering cider and eating their crêpes at the bar. That was my first really concrete vision—but, of course, I needed investors, and that meant I needed a business plan.

My friend Harry Weininger was my only businessman friend (he ran a carpet shop across the street from David's print shop), so I asked Harry if he would help me come up with the business plan. He took a look at the space and said, "Alice, you will never, ever, *ever* make any money doing this here." You can't make enough money off of crêpes, he told me, because they're too affordable. And plus, I wanted an environment where people would sit around, hang out, and talk—so there would be no turnover! I was planning to sell something for nothing, then ask people to hang around and never leave—that's how keen my business sense was.

As for the cider, I wanted to import that cider that I'd loved when I was with Sara in Brittany and Normandy. Only when I investigated how to import it did I find out it was *hard* cider, not regular. Somehow as I'd been drinking it, I never realized it had alcohol. No wonder I liked it so much; no wonder Sara and I had always fallen asleep after lunch.

Cider wasn't the only beverage I needed to educate myself about. I had had a lot of wine in France, but I didn't know very much about it until I started going to the wine shops in San Francisco. Obviously I wanted only French wine—but the Bay Area supermarkets only had jugs like Wente Brothers and Almaden. So I spent a lot of time hanging out in wineshops, which also felt a little bit like being in France. I really didn't know what I was looking for, but I was very curious about all of it.

That's how I met Paul Draper, who was working at Esquin Imports, a wineshop in downtown San Francisco that started in 1951. Esquin was like a library of wine: tall narrow shelves, with wines all the way up to the ceiling. Paul quickly became a friend; he was the most wonderful, handsome wine guy, and years later he started his own winery, Ridge Winery. I explored the shop with Paul, looking at all the bottles, and then he would tell me stories about them and choose the bottles for me—he loved that I had an interest in French wine.

Around that time I met Kermit Lynch, a rock musician and salesman for the *Berkeley Barb*, a notorious underground local newspaper (where Tom was the film critic at the time), who was just starting to import wine from France. A little later he opened a French wineshop on San Pablo Avenue in Berkeley, and we became really good friends. He was a Francophile, too, of course. We would go have lunch at this affordable little restaurant La China Poblana next door to his shop. I'd look out the window to a nondescript doughnut shop that was across the street and think, *We're having* the *most delicious lunch with* the *most delicious wines, and it costs practically the same as eating at that doughnut shop. It's so civilized here with Kermit, and that place across the street is a whole other world.* It made me want to lure people away from the fast-food franchises that were growing up all around Berkeley.

Kermit taught me all about terroir, growing the right varietal of grape in the right place, and trying not to get too much in the way of the winemaking. Terroir was about allowing the grape to be all it could be, bringing out the character of the place where it was grown, not trying to manipulate the wine too much by blending it. It was about letting the ingredients speak. That idea really influenced me in my thinking about organic farming, too, later on. And terroir wasn't just about rarefied wines; Kermit was always trying to find reasonably priced, authentically made regional wines, not these fancy ones that I couldn't afford.

Kermit showed me early on that you have to learn about wine by going to a vineyard. You do. If I had a cooking school, I'd do the same thing: I'd have everyone in the garden for six months, no cooking—just being in the garden, working with the farmer, planting and growing and harvesting. Then the second part would be coming inside and looking at and learning about the vegetables. The third part would be making something and serving it at the table. It's the same with wine. The best way to learn is to be involved with the grape harvest, watch when it's being put in the barrel, smell it, see the crush, taste the changes, observe how it matures, follow it.

I've witnessed that many times at many vineyards over the years, but the most special for me has always been Domaine Tempier. Kermit was the one who imported the wines of Lulu and Lucien Peyraud, and over time I became like a member of their family. I'm a lifelong drinker of their Domaine Tempier rosé. At the end of every grape harvest at Domaine Tempier, they set the long table outside under the arbor with at least twenty places, invite all the people who helped pick the grapes, and serve a big celebratory bouillabaisse. We always taste the current vintage first, then go back and taste the older bottles. It's an important ritual: being there on the land, drinking the wine from grapes you can reach out and touch.

*I will always remember one time, in the late 1970s, when I was traveling in Burgundy with Marion Cunningham and Cecilia Chiang. Cecilia owned the Mandarin Restaurant in San Francisco and was one of the few women I knew who ran a successful restaurant. They were my pals, Marion and Cecilia—I was in my late twenties, and they were in their early fifties, so they felt like big sisters. One afternoon we ate at a very fancy three-star restaurant in Burgundy, Chez la Mère Blanc. Fantastic wines, fantastic food, just the three of us.*

*At the beginning of the meal, the waiters came over, ready to pour the champagne, and Marion said in her inimitable, willful way, "No champagne. I'd like a cup of coffee!" Straight to the waiter, in English.*

*I was dying of embarrassment, and I said, "Marion, you cannot ask for coffee."*

*"But I want a cup of coffee, Alice!" she replied. Marion was an alcoholic and couldn't drink, so, of course, I didn't want her to actually drink the champagne—I just wanted her to let them bring it to her, to save face. Cecilia even got into it—she was normally above the fray, but here she was on my side.*

*But Marion insisted on her coffee. I was so mortified that I drank way too much wine at lunch, to compensate. Afterward I announced, "Let's go visit the vineyard where this wine comes from!" It was from Domaine de Montille, the vineyard of Hubert de Montille; Hubert sold his wine to Kermit, and I thought their Volnay was sublime. Kermit had encouraged me to go see Hubert while we were in Burgundy, though I'd never met the man and hadn't told him I was planning on coming. Marion was the driver, of course, since she was the only one who was sober, so we drove on over to the vineyard and rang the bell on the gate, and I yelled out, "I'm a friend of Kermit Lynch! We just had your wine!"*

*Hubert de Montille came to the gate to let us in, with shaving cream on and holding his shaving brush, like a character from an old French film. I don't know what we must have looked like to him: a beautiful Chinese woman and two Americans on his doorstep, one very tall and the other very short, showing up out of nowhere. But he knew Kermit, so he said, graciously, "I'll take you for a tasting in the cave." Marion, by this point, was at the end of her rope—here we were after our long lunch of drinking, and we were going to drink yet more wine? Hubert washed off his shaving cream and took us down into the cave.*

*I was really kind of drunk by this point. But Hubert was saying, "Let's taste these! All of these!" And so, of course, we did. With wine after wine, Cecilia was so right on—she didn't know a single name of any of them, but somehow she could taste the difference between each one, which one was the older vintage, which was younger, all the nuances, everything. And Hubert was so impressed with her palate that he said, "I'm going back into the cave to get the 'fifty-threes out!" By that point, I couldn't have taken another sip without falling to the ground. I have no idea how the '53s were, none.*

*Through it all, Marion was her gracious self, allowing us to do it. I have a picture of myself walking in the vineyard afterward—I was wearing an embroidered summer shift dress I still have, and my clogs, with my hair braided and pinned up in the back. I felt I had to survey the land after I drank the wine. I might not have been able to really taste the wine in that moment, but I felt so happy to be walking among the grapevines; wine comes alive when you have a sense of time and place, and when you understand the spirit of the winemaker.*

I thought a lot about a restaurant I knew from my trip in 1965, a place that was across the street from the Les Halles market: Au Pied de Cochon. Outside, they sold oysters to go, and inside, on the ground floor, you could stand at the bar and have the *menu du jour*—a glass of wine, an onion soup,

a *blanquette de veau*. Or you could go upstairs and have an elegant dinner with a white tablecloth. I thought, *This could be
wonderful here: it's a food shop, it's a café, it's a restaurant.* But I
didn't think I was capable of an à la carte dinner menu. With
an à la carte menu, you need to have more food on hand
because you don't know what people are going to order.
I wanted the food to be alive and perfect every night, and I
didn't want to have to keep food over from one day to the
next. So I thought, *We'll just have a fixed-price dinner menu that
changes every day, like at the neighborhood restaurants in Paris.*

I will say I was deflated by Harry's evaluation of my
crêperie. I wanted to do a restaurant that was small and
manageable, and I knew I could do a crêperie like that, but
the crêperie was off the table. We kept looking at buildings
that were much larger than I thought I could handle on my
own. I didn't feel nervous until I started thinking about
signing a lease and having to raise the money to open. I was
walking right up to the door of this big thing I wanted to do,
looking across the threshold, and seeing that it was going to
become real. And all of a sudden I realized it might be bigger
than I could imagine doing by myself, and I started getting
cold feet: *Where am I going to get the money? Who's going to help
me run it?* It all looked so much bigger than the little crêperie
I'd been thinking about in the beginning.

I didn't see much of Charles and Lindsey when I was dating Tom—I'd go over there sometimes, but never with Tom.
When David and I didn't get married, it had broken up our

foursome, Charles and Lindsey, David and me. They were *really* good friends with David and lived on the other side of town, so we weren't hanging out as much as we once had. But we were still close, and in 1970, when the conversation started up in earnest about the restaurant, I *knew* Lindsey and I were going to open it together. *She* didn't know, but *I* did! I did think the moment might be right for her, though: she had spent a decade raising their three kids, and Charles was very supportive of her getting out there and working again.

I have no memory at all of how I finally convinced Lindsey to join me, and neither does she; I have a tendency to recruit people to the cause, and I suppose she never really said no. Lindsey had a very classic aesthetic that I knew I wanted in the restaurant, whatever it was going to be. She made her fruit tart the way it'd been made for centuries, not changing it to be modern but making it meticulously, exactly the way they made it in Paris—where it looked like it came right out of a painting.

I looked for another person who could cook—I was *way* too afraid to shoulder all the cooking myself. Lindsey was an incredible baker and home cook, but she didn't know what she was getting into—she baked pies in a little oven and made them two at a time. Neither of us had any idea what it meant to be a restaurant cook—how could we have? We didn't even know what we didn't know. I was getting very nervous, and Tom, ever the great connector, said, "Oh, I'll find somebody for you!" He understood that I needed a

partner who had the chops, and he found Paul Aratow, an as-
piring filmmaker who was the cameraman for Agnès Varda's
documentary on the Black Panthers. Paul was a really good
Italian cook, and he did help me. I believed in his instincts.

Tom would take me to Paul's house and he'd make meals
for us. I was so impressed that Paul had a whole collection
of copper pots, not just the little saucepans but the really
big ones for making soup—and that he made his pasta by
hand. *Pasta alfredo* was his specialty, and he made a beautiful risotto, too. I tried that risotto, and right away I knew
I trusted him. Paul was not a professional, but I thought
he had great taste as a cook. And he talked a lot about how
he would be doing most of the cooking at this restaurant
we were going to open. And that *was* what I wanted; I had
a clear idea of what I wanted the cooking to be, but I didn't
think I could execute it all myself. So many other aspects of
running a restaurant also interested me. I knew I'd be good
at the hospitality part, getting people to the table, making
the table look beautiful—I wasn't worried about that. But
I didn't know whether I could actually be in a kitchen full-
time. It was the difference between cooking for eight people
and cooking for one hundred. I was really overwhelmed by
that, and Paul was flamboyantly self-assured: "I can do that.
Of course. *Pas de problème!*" His response to everything was
like that: "Don't worry about it! Let's just get to the restaurant supply place and start buying pots!" (To his credit, Paul
was usually the one to pay for these shopping sprees. If it

had just been me, I probably would've tried to collect all our cooking supplies from the flea market.)

It must seem strange that when I finally got close to opening this restaurant I'd been dreaming of for years, I chose not to be in the kitchen. But even though I was a waitress at the beginning, I was always thinking of the whole restaurant as a piece. In that way, it didn't matter where I was, because I was psychologically in the kitchen the whole time—I've never *not* been in the kitchen in my head. What drives the restaurant is the fine-tuning of the food, and I was intimately involved in that. I've always had great respect for cooks who can get the food to the place it needs to be, who are forever pushing that envelope, self-examining, thinking about food all the time the way I was. I think that was part of my bond with Jeremiah Tower, when he was the chef a little later on—we were both continually looking for better ingredients, better techniques, better ways to put a menu together. Even when I was waiting tables, I was thinking about who made each part of the meal, how the customers were responding to the food, what the room felt like—because when it all came together, it was magic. My role was not exactly that of an executive chef—it was more like a film director. I knew whom I wanted to cast in the role of the cook at the spit, who should play the role of the saucier, who was right for the role of the host welcoming people at the door.

Paul Aratow's vision for this restaurant was bigger than mine. He embroidered on my idea and was thinking more about La Coupole, a gigantic brasserie at Montparnasse in Paris that was open all hours. *Everybody* went to La Coupole, filmmakers, artists, movie stars; it was a place where people went to be seen, and I'm sure Paul was thinking about that atmosphere, too. Paul wanted our hours to be seven a.m. to two a.m., seven days a week. When somebody has that type of confidence, they carry you along with them—and at that particular moment, I didn't have any. His vision of the restaurant was basically to be all things to all people, and I was swept up in it.

From the start, I had never imagined anything more than a tiny little dining room that seated forty people, like the Quest. That model of one person in the kitchen was comprehensible to me. But when Paul and I started talking about those places in Paris, I just went into that fantasy. I thought, *We* do *need a café that serves breakfast and lunch and is open late into the night, we* do *need a patio out front, we* do *need this, we* do *need that.* Once again I was getting engulfed in another person's passion—and I was relieved to have someone else take the lead. The one thing I never let go of was the fixed-price dinner menu that would change daily. That was my vision, and it was nonnegotiable. And thank God I did, because it became the hallmark of Chez Panisse.

At that point, we didn't even know where we were going to get our food—it wasn't part of the conversation. Provenance wasn't something we worried about back then. We just assumed we'd order from the food distributors that other

French restaurants in San Francisco used, and it was a given that great ingredients would come. I was naïve enough to think that if we just followed in the footsteps of good French restaurants like La Bourgogne, and worked within their systems for getting ingredients, the raw materials would all be delicious. (I had a lot to learn—they were importing Dover sole from Europe and foie gras from Bordeaux.) What I was insistent upon was simplicity. What I was after more than anything was taste.

I never had a doubt in my mind that if we made really good food, people would want to come and eat there. It was nonnegotiable that it had to taste right, the way I imagined it in my mind. Taste was what won people over—I was sure of that. I didn't know then that the *really* good taste that I was after came from ingredients supplied by the organic farmers who were doing the right thing, the farmers who were taking care of the land and working with the old-fashioned, flavorful heritage varietals of fruits and vegetables, picking them at the moment of ripeness. In the years to come, following taste would lead me to the doorsteps of those organic farmers. I believe now that 90 percent of taste comes from an understanding of what seed should be planted in what place, how to care for the plant, when to pick it, and how quickly to eat it.

*I was thinking about Bordeaux recently, and what constitutes a First Growth designation for a wine, the Premier Cru classification.*

*How do they decide which wine deserves that highest designation? It all has to do with terroir. If a particular grape varietal is planted on a certain hillside and is tended in a certain way, you get a transcendent result. I was thinking that there must be a similar Premier Cru for peaches. There's a terroir for peaches, where if the right varietals are planted in the right spots, they can be the greatest peaches of all—like a Suncrest peach in August from Mas Masumoto's farm in the foothills of the Central Valley, or an O'Henry peach from Frog Hollow Farm in Brentwood. It's a combination of varietal and terroir and, obviously, a farmer who knows exactly the right moment to pick them. It's like Montessori, in some ways: create just the right creative, beautiful environment for each particular boy or girl, and he or she can grow into, you know, a Suncrest peach! Or an O'Henry—or a Fay Elberta!*

*The really interesting part for me is that there are so many microclimates and just as many varietals as there are microclimates. Farmers engaged in this process are calculating all the intricacies themselves: "That type of strawberry in the southeast corner of the field tasted best, so next year I'm planting more of those over in that corner." Carlo Petrini, founder of the international Slow Food movement, calls farmers the intellectuals of the land—when they're in the right understanding and frame of mind, they're doing it almost subconsciously. What's endlessly fascinating to me about cooking and eating is the biodiversity of the planet. The depth of the abundance of the earth. I'll never be able to comprehend it. Nobody can. And that's the tragedy of fast food—everything in this country changed with* fast food. We wanted shippability, we wanted year-round availability, we wanted food for cheap. And when you achieve all that, you take away everything—you lose touch with nature, and you exist in a hollow place, devoid of beauty and nourishment.

The truth is, I'd much rather feed people this idea than talk about it. When Bill Clinton was president, I wanted most of all for him to come to Chez Panisse so I could give him a peach at the end of his meal. I really wanted to serve him the right peach for the right moment in time; I was hoping it could focus his attention on the perfection of the fruit. I wanted him to be seduced by it, to be awakened and say, "I've never had anything like this!" I felt Clinton could be changed if he tasted the perfect peach, that he would get this idea about terroir and varietal and biodiversity without words—words are too limiting. I wanted to get to him through all his senses. Taste is an incredibly strong sensation—it's deeper than language. So are touch and smell. And it's very hard to reach people if they can't connect with all their senses. The only way I can know whether somebody is really listening, really getting it, is when he or she is eating.

And the great irony: the one time Clinton spontaneously came to the restaurant, in the beginning of August one year during his presidency, it was just a little too early for the Suncrest peach. Instead, I gave him a Gravenstein apple. But he didn't want it—he wanted the blackberry ice cream.

When I saw the house for sale at 1517 Shattuck Avenue, I thought right away, *Oh, this is possible*. I already knew the neighborhood so well, close to where David and I had lived, in the same block as the original Peet's Coffee and the Cheese Board Collective. It was a neighborhood where people were already selling good food, which heartened me.

Bob Waks and Sahag and Meg Avadisian had started the Cheese Board in 1967, four years before Chez Panisse opened—and oh God, yes, I was aware of it from the beginning. I was on the hunt for real food, and this shop was right near David's house, just down the block from the original Peet's Coffee. The Cheese Board was a workers' collective, a tiny hole-in-the-wall European cheese shop. Everybody who worked there got paid the same amount, which I loved, and that was what eventually convinced me that I should pay everyone five dollars an hour at the restaurant. I was so happy to finally have a European-style cheese shop in Berkeley; I knew what a real little cheese shop could be like, since we used to go to every *fromagerie* in Paris. And just like the shops in Paris, the Cheese Board educated all of us about cheese— you could taste little samples, so you learned about different flavors and textures and ages. From the moment it opened, I bought all my cheese there, and it influenced me when it came to deciding on 1517 Shattuck; I liked the idea of having our restaurant in that company.

The building at 1517 Shattuck Avenue was pretty ordinary looking: an old plumbing shop from the 1930s, with all kinds of pipes out front left over from the previous owners. But it was a house! A two-story house with a little back cot-

1517 Shattuck Avenue.

tage in the small yard behind it. It was an unusual choice, but it reminded me of the Gibson House in Bolinas. I thought, *Oh my God, maybe we really* could *do it in a house!* It was for sale for $32,000. I couldn't figure out how to buy it outright, but I asked the real estate agent if we could get a lease with an option to buy. That's what we eventually did: about three years later we bought it for $28,000. It was the best financial decision I've ever made, getting that lease to buy. Chez Panisse would have gone under if we'd had to pay rent—we were saved many times over by that.

I asked everyone I knew for money—Greil Marcus, a local music critic friend of Tom's who'd impressed me because he actually owned his own home; a few unnameable dope dealers; my parents. My parents offered to mortgage their house to loan me the money to open the restaurant. I loved that they wanted to do that. I figured that if all else failed, we could sell the house that the restaurant was in, so they'd get their money back. That way I felt I wasn't taking such a gigantic risk—or at least, I didn't think so. But, of course, I also thought that if it could get off the ground, it was going to work, absolutely. When they gave me the money, they made me feel, as they always did, that if it didn't come back to them, it didn't come back. And that was okay. I'm forever grateful that they did that—it wasn't just the money, it was knowing that my parents believed in me.

I had a long history of asking my parents for money. In every single letter I wrote them when I was in Europe in 1965, I asked them to send me twenty dollars. I was shameless: "Can I have money for the boat ride to Amsterdam?" Or "Could I have money for a new coat? All the Frenchwomen look so chic and I look like a Russian immigrant." Things like that.

It was unusual to be so close to your parents in the late 1960s and early '70s. Most young people seemed alienated from the generation that came before them. But then, as I said, my mother was always a radical. In 1970 my parents were living in Ann Arbor but were getting desperate to move out of the Midwest. My father started Organization Dynamics, a consulting company for businesses, and one of his business partners, Ray Miles, was at UC Berkeley, which was how they ended up moving here. But they really moved here because my mother wanted to, passionately. And what my mother wanted, she got, almost always. She was an old lefty, so coming to Berkeley was like coming to Mecca. She was never aggressive about it, but she was steadfast. By the time the restaurant opened, my parents were up in the Berkeley Hills, and they never left.

My mother also wanted to be nearer to me and my sisters Laura and Susan—that was the other big reason they came to California. None of my sisters were around during the planning of the restaurant. Ellen and her family were back from Vietnam and living in the Midwest, and Susan and Laura, though in the Bay Area, were in their separate orbits, and at that moment it felt like the four of us didn't have much in common. But I was busy at the time and, in all honesty, not paying much attention to my family. In the 1970s Susan and Laura were both in the counterculture but were making different choices than I was. Not that my choices were better—theirs were just different. They weren't involved in politics the way I had been.

Laura was part of the back-to-the-land movement. She was very beautiful, with long brown hair like Joni Mitchell and hazel eyes and a lovely, gentle demeanor. She was a wonderful painter and had studied art at UCLA—she made wild charcoal sketches and oil paintings, like a life-size portrait of herself (in the nude!) holding hands with Gary Cooper in cowboy attire. But after three years, she had to drop out of college and move back home because she got very sick with hepatitis. After she recovered, she moved to Berkeley in 1969 and reconnected with a high school sweetheart, John, got pregnant, and married him. A year or two later they really dropped out. They bought twenty acres of land in Mendocino, way out in the woods, dug their own well, and built their own house from recycled wood. She made all her bread from scratch—she was an excellent self-taught cook—grew all her own vegetables, had chickens and bees, and bartered with neighbors for other necessities. And all this with no electricity! They lived off the land and off the grid for five years.

*Laura has always been amused by the fact that I visited her up in Mendocino once, after the restaurant had been open a year or two, and she and I had an argument about whether organic was better than conventional. Laura was on the organic side, but I was still suspicious of it at the time—I had a vision of the beat-up, bruised organic vegetables sold at the co-op that weren't grown for taste or beauty. I understood the philosophy of organic farming, that it was better for the planet, but at that point the produce didn't taste or look good—yet.*

Tom knew Laura a little bit, and he knew Susan, too—he called Susan "Suey," our childhood nickname for her. She was the true redhead of the family, with thick wavy hair, blue eyes, and an ethereal look. Where Laura was laid-back,

Laura, Susan, me, and Ellen, circa 1970.

Susan was a little more outgoing. She had been the Beatles fanatic growing up—her whole room in Los Angeles was plastered with posters of them, and she loved all four of them with equal fervor. She had an unswerving optimism and idealism; the *all you need is love* ethos of the counterculture was what resonated with her and still does. When I was working to open the restaurant, Susan was living in Mill Valley at a time when it was *really* hippie. She immersed herself in that culture, and we didn't see much of each other for a while; Mill Valley was another world, and I was in a world of my own across the bay, starting the restaurant.

*Later Susan worked at the restaurant for eight years. She had a lot of musical talent—she played the piano wonderfully—and always had musicians around. She had a challenging relationship with one musician, a rock 'n' roll drummer, that was so hard for me to watch. One night this drummer showed up at the restaurant drunk and was giving her a terrible time. I was furious about the way he was treating my sister. I took him out of the restaurant, and then I just punched him in the face. I'd never done that before, and I've never done it since. I know violence is not the answer, it never is. But I was defending my sister.*

Even though my sisters and I didn't see much of each other during the planning of the restaurant, it didn't feel like a rift—we were raised with a certain familial looseness. My parents never made us feel constricted by an obligation to family; it was kind of a beautiful thing. My sisters felt the same way, more or less—we loved each other, but we weren't made to feel guilty if we couldn't see each other at every Christmas and Thanksgiving. It was a very different philosophy about family than a lot of people had, and a liberating one. My parents always gave each of us the message: "Do what you *like* to do." It's amazing to realize that you can create more than one family—you can have your biological family and also your chosen family of very close friends. What allowed us to go off and choose our own families was the confidence that my parents loved each other and that they loved all four of us the same. That was the greatest gift.

# CHAPTER 12

# Pagnol

"Alice, *these* are the films you're going to love. You've *got* to see them on the big screen."

Tom took me a lot to the Surf Theater in San Francisco to see movies, way out in the Sunset district. It was an independent neighborhood cinema run by Mel Novikoff, who

Tom said had great taste. After going out there a few times, I understood exactly what he meant. We went there for many films, but the most important ones for me were Marcel Pagnol's trilogy *Marius*, *Fanny*, and *César*. They're long films from the 1930s and very slow moving; you'd see one one night, then go for the second the next night, and the third the next night after that. We made a pilgrimage to the Surf Theater every night, and we'd talk about the films the whole way home. The screenings were sparsely attended, but Martine and Claude came with us; they had seen the films before. And Claude was just like a character out of the films; he looked almost as if he'd been drawn by the illustrators who made those old movie posters. And just like the Pagnol characters, Claude was a bon vivant, a raconteur, always having a glass of something while he talked. Martine and Claude both loved the films, of course.

Right away I liked these movies. After we saw the first one, *Marius*, I knew I was coming back the next night, no question. I just remember crying and crying about the characters and their lives. I could barely understand French, and certainly not Provençal French, so I had to read the subtitles—but it didn't stand in the way for me. There were hilarious scenes and heart-wrenching ones. It felt like the same complete immersion as the Gorky experience I'd had in Hampstead. Pagnol used a troupe of actors in many of his films, and *all* the same people were in this trilogy, so you got to know them really well—they felt like old friends by the end. The acting was exaggerated, a little melodramatic, but effective, almost like stage acting, and it really worked for me. The South of France, the harbor of Marseille, Fanny flirting with her customers to sell her oysters. It was romantic in that way.

The trilogy is a love story; at the heart of it is a love affair between Marius, the bartender's son, and Fanny, the girl who sells her oysters in front of the bar. Initially it made me want not so much to cook as to marry a Frenchman—just not one who would then abandon me and go off to sea, as Marius does! But the story is always circling around food: they're sitting at a bar, drinking a pastis, steaming up a bowl of mussels. And it shows a certain way of living—I really got that the three movies are parables about country values versus city values and a dying way of life: cards in the afternoon, a game of *pétanque*. I wanted to live in those films. There was a certain tenderness to the characters: Panisse is Marius's father's best friend, an older man who's successful in his sail-making shop. When Fanny gets pregnant with Marius's son, and Marius leaves her and goes to sea, Panisse offers to marry Fanny, so she won't lose respect. I loved that.

I connected to Pagnol, too, because our lives in Berkeley *were* a little like that already: we sat around playing cards, drinking pastis, talking and philosophizing, having love affairs. And in the end, our way of living fed into the idea of the restaurant, having a bar where people would gather, connect to each other, and live with a spirit of camaraderie around the table. I wanted to invite more people into that world. And maybe I responded because life in Provence was earthier than in Paris, and very sentimental. I did like the Parisian scene, of course—La Coupole, Au Pied de Cochon—but the Provençal life really moved me. Claude and Martine were from there, too. I hadn't even really spent time in Provence at that point, but Martine's cooking was steeped in that tradition: the mesclun salad with wild rocket, the dishes with beautiful olive oil, the anchovy paste, the roasted red peppers.

*I wasn't the only one obsessed with the Pagnol films. After the restaurant opened, I met the legendary food writer and Francophile*

Filmmaker Marcel Pagnol with his troupe of actors
and collaborators, circa 1930.

*M.F.K. Fisher, who lived nearby in Glen Ellen. She was a very striking woman in her seventies, her gray hair tucked back into a French roll. She had great eyebrows—she was beautiful, both as a younger woman and as an older woman. I think she identified with me because I was a young cook who was a woman, very intense and serious, running a restaurant. She was interested in Marcel Pagnol, and one time Tom and I took Pagnol's film,* The Baker's Wife, *up to show her. We would take those films everywhere and make a party out of it. We showed one reel, and it was magical, but then everyone was so tired (and we had drunk so much wine) that we left the second reel with her. We could never get that second reel back, for years and years! The idea was always that we'd come back and show the other reel at some point, but it never seemed to happen. And we aren't talking videotapes, we're talking about giant 16 mm reels—as big as serving platters.*

*Years later I went up to M.F.K.'s home in Glen Ellen with the writer Diane Johnson and thought I could finally retrieve my* Baker's Wife *reel. I thought she was going to be cooking for me, but when I arrived, she had the table set, and it was very clear, immediately, that she was not planning on cooking herself. I had brought some small gifts—a loaf of bread, some wild mushrooms, a handful of figs, a bottle of rosé, some beautifully colored eggs. But I was planning to give them to her, not to make anything with them! As soon as I realized she expected me to cook, I improvised this whole meal—I did wild mushrooms on toast with scrambled eggs and herbs. I just started cooking and said things like "Oh! I forgot! Do you have any butter or olive oil I could borrow? Or maybe some garlic?" As if I'd*

*simply neglected to pack it. I never let on, and she never knew. And,*
*of course, in my confusion, I completely forgot to pick up the reel.*

I saw the Pagnol films right around the time we were trying to dream up a name for the restaurant. We weren't sure
yet what to call it, but we knew what we wanted the tone of
the place to be: a place to gather, a place that had a bar and a
fixed-price menu. Initially, I experimented with calling it Le
Métro and having a design based on the Art Nouveau style
of the Paris Métro—David even did some artwork for it. I
asked everyone what they thought of this idea, ran around
getting input from all my friends, as I always do. But once
I fell in love with the Pagnol films, we riffed on names from
them: Chez Fanny, Chez César, Chez Marius.

Tom was the one who said it should be Chez Panisse,
because the warmhearted Panisse is the only character in
the story who made any money! And then I found out that
*panisse* is also the French word for the little chickpea fritters
made in Provence. So it was settled: Chez Panisse. At that
point, Paul Aratow was so overwhelmed with construction
and equipping the kitchen that I figured the last-minute
change didn't matter to him much. I had gone into the whole
restaurant endeavor with more of a Parisian mentality, but
the name "Chez Panisse" ended up invoking the South of
France—a decision that would shape the feel of the restaurant in a way I'd never imagined.

TOUS LES JEUDIS

# FILM
# COMPLET

15 FRANCS • 30 PAGES

# La femme
## DU
# BOULANGER

:CHEZ:PANISSE:
CAFE & RESTAURANT
1517 SHATTUCK BERKELEY 94709
548·5525
CAFE UPSTAIRS APERITIFS WINE BEER GUINNESS ESPRESSO
DESSERTS PASTRIES SUNDAES

# Opening Night

So many things were going on in the months before we opened. We didn't have much money, so we were doing a lot of the work ourselves. Paul brought in his brother and a few others to help do the construction and get everything permitted with the city: stoves with hoods, a brick patio, a cement retaining wall out front. In order to make the retaining wall look a little less cement-like, Paul's brother took one of the old doors from the house and pressed it into the wet cement, which gave it a geometric pattern. We built and installed a swinging door between the kitchen and the dining room, stripped and refinished the old hardwood floors and redwood baseboards, and repainted inside and out. The paint colors were Martine's domain; of course, she approved of Chez Panisse right from the beginning and loved the idea that we were devoting ourselves to making an authentic little French restaurant. Lindsey was going back and forth between her house and the restaurant every day on her bicycle, and had staked out the back cottage behind the restaurant for making tarts—that was *her* domain. It was a little furnished cottage with a conventional stove, so in some ways it wasn't that different from the way Lindsey cooked at home.

*When Lindsey started cooking at Chez Panisse, she still made her tarts one by one, just as she had for her family. As it turned out, she brought the best qualities of home cooking into a professional kitchen and helped to shape it. She was so detail-oriented and had such a fine palate. She would make a crème anglaise or a tart over and over until it was exactly right. She worked completely differently from me, even though I was a home cook, too—she took notes, was methodical, and could actually remember what she had done the last time! I loved that Lindsey never wasted anything, either. She'd use tiny pieces of paper to write her notes—addenda to her recipes, or messages to people in the kitchen—then she'd save those scraps, and the following day she'd write her next note on the opposite side of the paper. We were always finding Lindsey's well-worn bits of paper tucked around the kitchen.*

*Even as we started to get familiar with the pattern and flow of a restaurant kitchen, we never really became professionals. But in a way we changed the idea of what it was to cook in a restaurant—we did it so unconventionally that the unconventional became habit. We had a different rhythm. We didn't make ice cream ahead of time—we made it the day we served it, just as you would at home. And we didn't have anybody junior come in in the morning and do all the prep work so the chef wouldn't have to be concerned with the* "menial" tasks of chopping vegetables for the mirepoix or washing the salad. Everybody who cooked there did all his or her own prep work. That was very unusual, very nonprofessional. We would change the menu to accommodate food that had just arrived at the back door—if some beautiful raspberries appeared, we'd incorporate them right away, we wouldn't stick to a predetermined menu. And for that matter, we didn't have any recipes written down, except for Lindsey's pastries. It was always word of mouth among the cooks. There was a constant dialogue going on about how to prepare a dish: sometimes it had to do with the weather, or with someone's idea from the last time we cooked the duck. It was an ongoing conversation, always in process; we felt that if we stuck to a written recipe, it would be harder to use our minds in a flexible way that would allow us to make it better.

We didn't use machines—we hand-pounded the garlic for our vinaigrettes. (We did eventually admit we needed a blender to purée soups—before that, we used a hand mill.) The thing about it was that all those nonprofessional habits of ours made the food taste different—we didn't have any bad habits. We were never looking for the easiest way, we were looking for the best way—and very often it was actually the hardest way, but it didn't matter to us. And because we had only one menu every day—again, just as you would at home!—it focused our attention and pushed us to discover new ingredients. Every day we had to make the meal not only perfect but different from the days before, so we were forever on the hunt for ingredients that would surprise people. If we'd had an à la carte menu, I suspect we wouldn't have had the impetus to find

*new things out there in the world as rapidly. It all came from the*
*urgency of the single menu.*

The building wasn't a Victorian—that would have been my
dream—but I found an old Victorian stained-glass window with Martine in a salvage yard. It was rectangular with
reds and ochers and deep purples and had a big number in
it, 1803—it was clearly a street address that had once been
placed above the front door of a Victorian house. We installed it above one of the doors into the kitchen. It looked
great. Martine and I also found lots of old mismatched Art
Deco light fixtures, because they reminded me of the places
where I'd eaten in Paris, places from a certain time that had a
warm, golden, almost antique light to them. We were always
looking for little rose-colored lampshades, which I'd seen
in pictures in a book about the old French restaurant Maxim's; I loved that book, *Chez Maxim's*. And I also thought a lot
about what César Ritz had done when he opened the Carlton
in London: he took a woman around with him from room to
room, sat her down next to the lamp in each room, and if the
light made her look beautiful, then that was the right one for
the room. *That* was what I wanted from my lamps.

*When I met Martine, lighting was her speciality—from the kinds*
*of bulbs she had in her house to the shades she made for her lamps.*
*When she went into a room, she would go around, turn on some*
*lamps and turn off others, light candles, and create this romantic*

space. I had that memory of the colored glasses on the windowsill at Aunt Ina's, and of going to see sunsets—my mother and Aunt Ina would take us out for drives to watch the sunset or to watch the full moon come up. But Martine was the one who really turned me on to lighting. I saw its magic, and ever since I've been obsessed—I know how light affects people's moods. Everyone I've ever worked with has been tortured by my obsession with lighting. I can always talk about it—the way I can always talk about lettuce. After forty-five years, I'm still working on the lighting at the restaurant—and everywhere else I go!

Sometimes in the evenings I walk upstairs into the café and am so disappointed to see the blinds pulled down on the porch windows, which look out to the west and to the sunset. I do not want those blinds down—when a Maxfield Parrish sunset is going on outside the window, you want that in the restaurant, that incredible golden light that affects people for an hour or two. To me that sunset is part of the ambience of the restaurant. It's not blinding sun—the sunset filters in through the little Art Deco lights at the top of the window-panes, which are made with a tinted rose-colored glass, and it brings that color and that warmth into the room. This Vermeer lighting streaming in makes everyone and everything look beautiful.

Martine also taught me that when you have light from only one source, especially from overhead, you create stark shadows. But you're trying to create a sort of uniform softness, so you need lights on the table, on the walls midway, and up above. It's very hard to have enough light on a tabletop without it being too harsh overhead—and in many restaurants, the light's too low, and you can't see the food on the plate well enough. We couldn't have candles that first night because we weren't allowed open flames, so we just had fixtures on the walls and up above; these days we have a little copper lantern on each table, with a glass-covered votive candle inside.

I want the light right in the kitchen, too—I don't want fluorescents, because they have a white glare that brings out the worst in people's complexions and feels so industrial. It's such a simple thing to light a candle—it changes the whole tone of an experience at a table. Almost more than anything else, I feel if I get the lighting right, I can change people's way of thinking, predispose them to let the experience wash over them. It's yet another inexpensive way to make a space beautiful.

I'm the only person at the restaurant who feels so intensely about the lights. And because the quality of the light changes throughout the day, I always have to be vigilant about it. I'm just as obsessed about firelight, too—we have fires at the restaurant not just for cooking but for the look of them and the light they give off. People know deep down inside themselves that firelight means comfort and food and warmth, all the things that fire brings. (When we first opened, there was a fireplace at one end of the dining room. Sadly, it never worked, but the mantel became the place where Carrie Glenn put her wonderful flower arrangements.)

I've always had mirrors in the restaurant, too—they are the great amplifiers of light. Pretty early on we installed big full-length mirrors upstairs, with gold sunbursts etched into them, very Art Deco, and they've been there for a long time—I got them at a junk shop in Oakland for ten dollars each. Years later I had smaller mir-

*rors made, about eight inches high and trimmed with redwood, that ring the perimeter of the dining room. They're placed just a little above table height to pick up the light from the candles on the tables. These distressed, smoky, rose-tinted mirrors were used in the dining rooms of fancy transatlantic ocean liners in the 1930s and '40s. It's a very subtle thing, but I was blown away by their effect when I first found them.*

In the chaos of the construction of the restaurant, David Goines started dating a printing student of his, Patty Curtan. Patty—who became a lifelong friend and collaborator—told me recently that the first time she heard my voice, she and David were working in his darkroom together. He was printing the very first menu for Chez Panisse, a vertical page with a curvilinear Art Nouveau design, with tall blue flowers in a geometric, formalized style. I came into the shop to ask him how it was coming along. She could hear my voice on the other side of the wall—the little baby voice I apparently use when I'm trying to get people to do something for me!

It meant a lot to me to have David play a part in this thing we were creating—I couldn't imagine anyone but him making the menu for the restaurant. After our breakup, I wasn't willing to let David go from my life—and truthfully, I never have, not him or any of the other men I've loved. It's so lucky that we managed to find our way to a friendship; it's the greatest thing to have someone you've been in love with who's still a friend. You become like family when that happens, you just know them so well. There were certainly rough months right afterward—it's painful to break up with anyone under any circumstance, and no matter how much it needs to happen, it's very sad. But somehow it was one of the best breakups. I think David and I had ended our relationship with enough care and forethought that we still had a lot of mutual respect and love for each other.

David printed that first beautiful menu, with room for me to write in the changing fixed-price meal every night. But remember, we were going to be open from seven a.m. to two a.m., and somehow we thought the rest of the menu would stay the same—we thought we knew what we'd be serving every day for breakfast and lunch. We dreamed up coffees and teas and crêpes for breakfast, eggs *en cocotte*, *omelette au fromage*. David printed hundreds and hundreds of copies of that menu, as if it were to be the menu of Chez Panisse forever. And, of course, it was obsolete before we even opened! (I *knew* we shouldn't have had any à la carte options!) What we were serving changed so quickly, even from morning to afternoon, that there was no way we could give David the information fast enough. When we finally opened, I ended up hand-calligraphing the whole menu myself, and we'd run it off on a copy machine at the drugstore down the street.

*Whenever we had a special dinner at Chez Panisse, we would print the menu letterpress, and we developed a great group of people who participated in designing those menus. Patty Curtan was one of those*

*artists—I responded to her aesthetic because besides being a meticu-*
*lous letterpress printer, she was also a cook and a gardener. She and*
*I got to know each other, and one night shortly after the restaurant*
*opened, when we were absolutely desperate for help in the dining*
*room, I called her and said, "Just put on a dress, and I'll pick you*
*up in fifteen minutes." Patty came and worked behind the bar. And*
*then I asked if she could come the next night, and the night after, and*
*the night after that . . . and that's how it began. She started at Chez*
*Panisse at twenty-one, and more than forty years later we're still*
*working together. Starting with the pasta book we published in the*
*1980s, Patty has designed and worked on every book we've done. Her*
*line drawings are so evocative, and a lot of her talent comes from her*
*incredible gardener-cook mind; she can pick a vegetable right from*
*the garden, at the height of its ripeness, and draw it perfectly. She*
*learned the elements of classic illustration and design so wonderfully*
*that now she can improvise with a lot of deftness.*

In the beginning I was always just trying to grab people to
work for us. It's how I operated, and it was sort of a counterculture way of doing things; if I saw a friend who needed
a job and had a talent and could do one thing—who could
draw beautifully, for example, or play the piano—I wanted
that precision in the kitchen, or I was applying it to how they
might operate an espresso machine. It was not about a job
description, it was about looking for interesting people who
could breathe life into the restaurant. And I always wanted
to work with people I really *liked*. I didn't want to be just in

a professional relationship, because it was—is—my whole life. I always wanted to be having a conversation with someone who inspired me the way César and Panisse did, when they gathered around playing cards in the movie *Marius*.

Before the restaurant opened, Bob Waks from the Cheese Board found some great people to work for us. He knew everybody around town—he was incredibly outgoing and wild and charismatic and funny, a talented amateur dancer and falsetto singer—he could get way up there at the end of a song. Bob was so endearing; I always felt like a party wasn't real if he wasn't there. When you were with him, you'd have this wonderful feeling that you were his best friend or his lover, the only person for him. When you were with him, you were *it*. And he gave everybody he knew that impression—he was totally enraptured with whomever he was with. It's a selfless, genuine personality trait that's a pretty amazing gift; there aren't too many people who have it. He always came through for you, and that's a rare thing. I always thought, *When I'm really sick and ready to leave the world, he's the person I'd want to take care of me*. I loved him and took practically every suggestion he gave me.

Sharon Jones had been living in a commune with Bob Waks; she was the first waitress I officially hired. When she arrived to apply for the job, I was in the back cottage conducting interviews. She was maybe twenty-five, wearing a purple and white gingham dance dress and brown cowboy boots, her curly hair in two little pigtails. She was *so* cute—

effervescent, with a huge smile. Sharon kept trying to tell me about her waiting experience—she'd been a Stouffer's girl and had waited tables in Cape Cod after college. But what really impressed me was what she looked like and the fact that she had just got back from traveling in Kathmandu. The interview lasted about thirty seconds—I hired her immediately. (She and I became best friends, we raised our kids together, and she's now the head of the board of directors of Chez Panisse.)

Jerry Budrick came in because of Bob Waks, too. A couple weeks before we opened, he showed up beautifully dressed for the interview, wearing a white shirt and a smart black vest, and he appeared very waiterly to me. He was so cool-looking and sophisticated, smoking his cigarette; I *believed*. He told me he'd waited on people at a restaurant in Austria. He pulled out his wallet, this fancy European leather wallet, and I hired him in half a second. He was cute, too. (Jerry later told me he'd wanted to help with the construction, too, since it was so obvious that we weren't going to meet our opening deadline.)

John Harris was another one of our first waiters who came through Bob. He was a writer, a former Cheese Board employee, and a friend of Bob's. He was a great lover of garlic and was known around the neighborhood as the garlic king. He'd written a book on garlic and liked to wear this big old garlic hat, like a chef's toque with a gigantic head of garlic at the top. He later convinced us to start our annual garlic festival. We also hired a woman from France to be a

Me, Lindsey, and Victoria planning menus, Richard Olney's
*French Menu Cookbook* in hand.

waitress: Brigitte Segal, a friend of Tom's. What could be
more perfect—an actual French person in the dining room!
Brigitte was tall with curly black hair, had a great figure, and
was incredibly sexy. This was long before I required uniforms. She always wore short, tight, tight dresses when she
was waiting tables.

What we were thinking about doing menuwise was pretty
straightforward. We were planning to make really simple
French country food, like roast chicken, or lamb with beans.
Paul was so overwhelmed with constructing the space that
in the final weeks before we opened, he had to hire another

cook: Victoria Kroyer, who was so talented in her home kitchen and had so much confidence. She was the same age as me, twenty-seven, had dark hair and dark eyes, was very buxom, and had a willingness to leap into the fray—she was just open to anything. The idea was that Paul would be the executive chef, and Victoria would be the main chef in the kitchen, though in the end Victoria shouldered a great deal more of the menu planning and cooking than Paul did.

Victoria was an incredibly hard worker, there from dawn to dusk. We understood each other, and I had a lot of respect for her, though we were both stubborn—two big personalities in a very small kitchen. What attracted me to Victoria was that we had the same vocabulary about food, the same intellectual interest. She had cooked a lot at home and was into making pâtés and sausages. (Later she opened up a fantastic shop across from Chez Panisse called Pig-by-the-Tail, the first charcuterie in Berkeley).

My best times with Victoria were when we were figuring out menus. She made great dishes like chicken *demi-deuil*—it means "in half-mourning," because black truffles are stuffed under the skin in a cream sauce. She also cooked celery root in various applications, like celery root soup and the classic celery root remoulade. She made ratatouille, and *frisée aux lardons* salad, and duck cassoulet, and *choucroute garnie*, a sauerkraut garnished with sausages. Victoria also made wonderful *rognons de veau*, veal sweetbreads browned in butter in a cast iron pan. She wanted all those innards, and she cooked them really well. Nobody was cooking recipes like that in the American mainstream, and, of course, Victoria and I absolutely adored that food. I never would have chosen them on my own, but I liked doing those sorts of classic, rustic French dishes.

*I've always liked the communal feeling of collaborating on menus with a chef, the give-and-take. That was another reason I'd shied away from being the sole person responsible for cooking: I wanted to be working and thinking and creating in the company of others—I didn't want to be on my own or in a vacuum. I was never looking to take away from a great cook who could do something perfectly, though. I'm willing to let go when a chef is in that place—if someone is in that zone, I don't want to disrupt it. When that's happening, they're leading a path through the woods, and I don't want to disturb their confidence.*

*In the mid-1970s I finally did move into working in the kitchen full-time, and by then I really knew what it was about—I understood what it was to make a salad for fifty. By that point, my anxiety about being in the kitchen had evaporated. I also had Jean-Pierre Moullé as the other chef in the kitchen then, and it was incredibly lucky that he was so talented.*

*When I was cooking in the restaurant kitchen, I liked the spontaneous calculations that were involved. I would always simplify as I went along. If I couldn't have complete control over those green beans, if it took too much focus to make them exactly the way I wanted them when I was cooking on the line, I'd simplify the cook-*

ing method. I'd strip down the dish to its most essential parts, the ones I knew I could get right. It's still so surprising to me that up in the café these days, they can have four or five beautiful, distinct elements on a plate. That's a lot of spoonfuls of ingredients that each have to be perfected, a lot of coordinating. Line cooks have become so much more skilled than I ever was.

I stayed in the kitchen for nearly seven years, from about 1976 to 1983, and in some ways I was relieved to get out of it. But I did love figuring out the intricacies of the menu as the day and night went on, incorporating new ideas that came to me as I was cooking. I miss that process of being deep in it. Even though I'm out of the restaurant's kitchen now, I still spend so much time thinking about ways to improve upon the food. The other night I cooked a risotto for friends at home but had forgotten some of my little tricks, and I was really unhappy with myself for not remembering. I didn't add quite enough stock and allowed it to cook down a bit too far. And to brighten risotto, I usually end with a little lemon rind, parsley, maybe even some finely minced garlic just before serving. But I forgot about all that! I agonized over those omissions all through the night. (I apologized to my friends the next morning; they graciously said they hadn't noticed.) For several weeks now I've also been worrying about the chicken al mattone that we make on the grill in the café; should we really be using chicken legs or just the chicken breast? It's so tricky to grill a chicken leg, because the little joints in the skin have a texture that can be chewy, without that perfect crispness to the skin. It's different when you cook it in a cast iron pan, because extra heat comes in from the sides of the pan—but with a *grill more air circulates, so it's hard to get the joints of the chicken leg cooked to that point of crispness.*

*That detailed calibrating of a dish is what I'm best at—helping refine flavors. I can always identify what's not quite right, and when I taste it, I have a vision in my mind of what it could become. But sometimes I can't quite identify exactly what it needs to get it there—it takes a conversation and a collaboration with someone else. I'm best as an editor of a dish. I know what the work of cooking is, and I can really fine-tune.*

Victoria had a master's from Berkeley in philosophy. I liked that—once again, no formal culinary training. Not that that mattered: I wanted people who had *some* cooking experience, but then Lindsey Shere had experience and was a non-professional, which meant she proceeded like a home cook. Despite our collective lack of professional qualifications, everyone was on the same page when it came to talking about food; we were Francophiles and understood the language of French food. We were intellectual gastronomes, if you will—Lindsey, Victoria, and Paul—and we all came from a well-read place. I had devoured *Larousse Gastronomique* and Richard Olney and Elizabeth David and M.F.K. Fisher and so many others. These writers all loved and celebrated France and French food, and they excited all of us. Our resident French aesthete, Martine, made the first sign for the restaurant, where we planned to post the new menu every day. It was about three feet tall, carefully hand-painted in a delicate, dreamy style. I loved everything about it and framed and hung it on a wire from the big bunya-bunya tree growing next to the restaurant entrance. (I didn't know then that bunya-bunya trees live to be six hundred years old; in their native Australia, they're considered to be sacred gathering places.) We didn't have anything that properly displayed the restaurant's name, so a couple of days before we opened, David chalked CHEZ PANISSE in two-foot-high Art Nouveau lettering on the wooden fence out front.

We put small palms on either side of the stairs outside the restaurant, the way a place like Maxim's would have potted palms in corners of the dining room. I'm a bit embarrassed to say I installed a trailing potted houseplant on a

pillar inside, next to the stairs that led up to the restrooms; that was a very late 1960s, early '70s thing to do. We had the mismatched plates and silverware that Jacqui, Martine, and I had found at the flea market. I had red-and-white-checked oilcloths—I would have got linen tablecloths, but in the end we couldn't afford them—and fresh flowers on the tables.

We had flowers at the restaurant from the moment we opened—I'd place them in little jars at each table. I did it myself until our florist Carrie Glenn arrived. I wasn't doing arrangements, really—just putting something like three tulips into a glass. It was very simple at the beginning. But even when money was really, really tight, I always found some for the flowers; I used to buy them from the flower shop on Ashby and Telegraph, where Carrie Glenn worked, down the street from our house on Dana Street. I became friends with her because she'd lead me to the flowers she liked best, which were always the most beautiful ones. I'd drive across town from Chez Panisse just to buy her flowers. And after a little while it was natural for her to come and arrange them at the restaurant.

*Carrie's arrangements were astonishing from the very beginning, and pretty soon I couldn't do without them. They were simply so, so much better than I could ever imagine doing myself. She brought a particular beauty into the restaurant that really pleased me. In the early days when I couldn't go out, when I was in the kitchen all the time, she brought nature into the dining room. We were lucky—she was a true artist. In the fall, she'd forage big branches of maple trees, these flames of color, or she'd incorporate fruit into her arrangements: wild blackberries, persimmons, Meyer lemons. I found them spectacular.*

*I'm still very self-critical about how I arrange flowers. I love to do it, but I fuss a lot, moving things around, changing the vases, feeling like I've never quite got there. I'm a wannabe florist, but I'm not patient enough. The way Carrie handled flowers was in another realm. She would go foraging to find flowers and branches and vines for her bouquets—sometimes in the middle of the night— harvesting them from trees and bushes all along the streets of Berkeley! She would meticulously take off the errant leaves, one by one. Pretty soon she started connecting with the local flower growers, too, just as we did with the farmers; her floral style influenced so many people around the country. I was always struck by how intricate and subtle her arrangements were. People would come into the restaurant just to see the flowers, then turn around and walk out.*

We started off with flea market dishware and used restaurantware, but I was always on the lookout for vintage Limoges china. In those first years, I'd get it wherever I could find it, dinner plates in sets of ten or twelve with matching dessert dishes. I made the poor dishwasher wash them all by hand. Needless to say, they still broke like crazy, and I eventually took the remaining Limoges dinner plates home. But the little dessert dishes, the mismatched six-inch plates, those lasted. They were the perfect size, and we used them

in so many ways all through the night, not just for dessert—
and the next morning poor Lindsey would have to hunt all
around the restaurant and patiently collect all the dessert
dishes we'd appropriated. The dishes have survived through
the years, and we still use them to serve candies at the end of
the meal. It's sort of a signature of Chez Panisse.

It's funny that music wasn't part of the restaurant when
it started. It really affected me, music—I spent so much time
focusing on it. Half my classes in college were about music:
one was entirely about Beethoven's symphonies, different
recordings of all his symphonies. I always tried to find the
right music for the right circumstance, and I couldn't listen
to the canned music that was omnipresent in restaurants.
The right music could bring everybody together when it
reinforced a harmonious gathering, but the wrong music
would interfere. And I just couldn't figure out what to play
in the restaurant. I thought about French restaurants that
never had music, and about how I didn't want to interrupt
the conversation at the table. I'd rather have no music than
the wrong music.

*A couple of years later, we all got into opera—that was our chef Jer-
emiah Tower's territory. He played a record of the incredible tenor
Jussi Björling singing in* Manon Lescaut. *In between seatings, it
would be blaring in the kitchen; Jeremiah played it over and over
until the grooves on the record wore out. And he played only the*

*very peak arias of Puccini, nothing less! But when we opened, we didn't have any music at all. What has finally ended up working in the dining room of the café upstairs is classic jazz from the 1950s. That's ironic, since it's exactly what I avoided listening to when I was younger.*

Tom and Martine and Claude and I all loved to play poker and Bourré over at our house. I don't know how I kept up the poker nights as I got deeper into the restaurant construction, but I managed because I loved playing with them so much. Martine and Claude had a friend named Jean Vatinel—we called him Vati—who worked for Mondavi, and sometimes he'd show up for our poker nights. Vati would bring wine for us to drink while we were playing. We drank the Mondavi gamay mostly—and around the time the restaurant was being built, he started bringing bottles of Mondavi's '68 cabernet sauvignon. Over the course of a poker evening, we'd drink our way through all the cheap wines he brought, and when he lost, he was forced to bring out that '68 cabernet. I realized later that it was sort of infanticide to drink the wine that young, but I loved that cabernet. Vati was such a good salesman that we bought Mondavi wine when we were close to opening. We couldn't afford the cabernet, but we bought their gamay and their *fumé blanc,* and also a 1959 Château Suduiraut, a Sauternes. Those were our only three wines on our first wine list, and we served them all by the glass.

It seems so strange that we had only three wines on our list, and that one of them was a Sauternes, a sweet wine that most people drink only after dinner. But I'd started drinking it along with Lindsey's desserts, and then Paul Draper had deepened my appreciation of it. And at that time, believe it or not, the greatest Sauternes in the world cost only $2.50 a bottle. One Sauternes was *really* expensive—Château d'Yquem—and that was $3.50 a bottle! I fell in love with all of them. They had a richness and a complexity that was so beautiful. In a good year, the great châteaux of Sauternes are just lovely—but the one that is always a little more lovely is Château d'Yquem. When I started figuring out wines for our list, I knew I needed a Sauternes, so I bought ten cases of the 1959 Château Suduiraut. I would have got the Yquem if I could, but I thought it was just too expensive. In retrospect, I really wish I had got that $3.50-a-bottle Yquem and that I still had some in my cellar today.

Francis Ford Coppola came over for one of our poker nights around that time; I served everyone a gratin of potatoes topped with anchovies before running back to the kitchen to finish up. Francis started eating and shouted out from the dining table, "Alice, you know, you should open a restaurant!" Tom said something to the effect of "Wait a couple weeks!"

In those weeks before we opened, Tom would get off work at the Telegraph Rep, come to the restaurant around nine or nine-thirty, and try to get me out of there to go home and rest. I'd say, "No, no, no, just a minute!"—he always came too early. He'd sit there waiting for me, drinking the glass of wine I'd bring him while I ran around figuring out what jobs needed to be done the next day; we never left before midnight. I'd wake up early the next morning, and he would beg me to stay in bed for just twenty-five seconds so that he could hold me. But I'd shoot out of bed. I knew if I stayed just twenty-five seconds, it wouldn't be twenty-five seconds, and I had no time.

Victoria, Lindsey, Paul, and I decided the opening night's menu would be *pâté en croûte*, duck with olives, and Lindsey's plum tart. I wanted *pâté en croûte* because it was one of the most successful, fanciest things I'd ever served at a dinner party. A couple years before, I had made a pâté with black truffles and pistachio nuts and served it with a special wine from Paul Draper, a 1953 Calon-Ségur. I'd got the recipe from Henri-Paul Pellaprat's *The Great Book of French Cuisine*; it was baked in a flaky pastry crust, then sliced. It was texturally great and felt elegant because it was encased in a rich, classic crust. Making any sort of pâté takes a lot of skill, and this recipe was particularly tricky—you had to taste the mixture before it went into the pastry crust, then cook it at the right temperature so the flavors married, and you still didn't know how it was going to turn out. Luckily the one time I had made it at home, I was successful, and my reaction was just "Oh my God!" It was like making a soufflé for the first time—there was magic in it. I knew Victoria had experience making pâtés, so I thought this *pâté en croûte* would be perfect—she could cook it the day before, and all we'd have to do that night was slice it.

As for the main course, I wouldn't have thought of duck on my own—I'd never even cooked it myself before—but Victoria knew how to roast duck, and I loved that she knew. Victoria and I agonized about the right olives to use with the duck: green or black? We didn't want them to be too pungent, and the black ones were oilier and stronger. We finally decided on Sicilian green olives, both for the color and for their mildness and ability to marry with the sauce. Lindsey's plum tart was a fait accompli—she knew how to make it, and she could make a lot of them. She had a whole dessert repertoire that we served at the restaurant for years and years. Plum tart, crème anglaise, and almond tart—those were her slam dunks.

I wanted to keep the dinner price low, though Paul lobbied for it to be higher. I just wanted all my friends to come, and I thought if it was too high, they wouldn't show up. We ended up deciding on $3.95 for the whole meal, which was pretty steep at the time.

By late summer 1971, it was clearly time to open—basically because we needed some money coming in. We had no test dinners; we just called our friends, told them what night to come, and opened cold.

That evening, August 28, 1971, was unusually warm, and we decided to put tables outside on the front patio so people could sit and have an apéritif before dinner. I wasn't cooking that first night—I was in the dining room; Victoria and Paul were in the kitchen, making duck with olives. We had got the ducks from Chinatown that morning, because construction was still going on right up until the very end, and there was nowhere to put them. We hadn't finished the construction upstairs—Jerry had been right that we couldn't make it in time—so we hung a curtain at the top of the staircase, and all the extra furniture and tools and building materials that didn't have places yet were stored up there. Just a few hours before dinner was to be served, Paul's brother Charles was in the kitchen setting up the prep counter for Victoria. One of Lindsey's biggest memories of opening night was having no electricity in the building until shortly before opening; I remember nothing about that—I was arranging things in the dining room in the daytime, so electricity wasn't critical for me.

A few things I do remember vividly. It was still light outside, and the first party, a man and a woman I didn't know, were coming in the front door for their reservation. I was wearing a vintage crocheted beige lace dress from Bizarre

Bazaar that fit like a glove and some little heels that matched; I remember feeling very self-conscious—*Do I look okay to be answering the door?* I was still tacking down the secondhand Persian carpet runner on the stairs as these people walked in. I wasn't nervous so much as obsessed—I needed *everything* to be done in a certain way before we opened, and the runner was part of it.

After that couple, it was practically all people we knew, a real Berkeley crowd. There was Phil Wood, a local publisher; rock critic Greil Marcus and his wife, Jenny; Danny and Hil-

A few hours before we opened.

ary Goldstine, two Berkeley sex therapists; my old friend Eleanor and her date Ronnie Davis, head of the San Francisco Mime Troupe; Jacqui West, wearing a beautiful emerald green vintage Chinese dress, with her husband, Skip; a little group of letterpress printers, including Bill Buckman and Greg Robb from St. Hieronymus Press, where David worked; and, of course, David and Charles, and Claude and Martine and their baby, Camille, in her vintage wicker baby carriage; my mother and my sister Laura, who was seven months pregnant.

And Tom, who had just come from filming George Jackson's funeral earlier that day. George Jackson was a member of the Black Panthers and had been shot to death by prison guards during an unsuccessful escape attempt. Huey Newton, the head of the Black Panthers, had called Tom and asked him to find a cameraman to film the funeral; Tom and his cameramen were the only film crew allowed in the church. It was a reminder to us that it was a dark time—we all felt like the counterculture was under siege. Students were being shot at Kent State, Robert F. Kennedy and Malcolm X had been killed—so many people had been assassinated. In some ways, Chez Panisse was born from the ashes, as many of the ideals we'd been fighting for were being destroyed.

The whole night was out of control. I didn't have any real conversations with anyone, I was just racing to get everything to the people eating. It took a rather long time for everyone to get served; Sharon kept refilling everyone's wineglasses so they wouldn't leave. She said that from the moment she walked in to work that first night, it smelled unlike any other restaurant she'd ever been in—it smelled like magic, she said. She had been planning on helping out for only two or three weeks before starting a teaching job, but on that opening night, she knew she wanted to stay and be part of it. And thank God she did!

I needed everyone who was in the dining room that night, this motley group of people who ended up working together. They were all charismatic and were all trying their best to make people happy. That night—and every night thereafter—our job was to convince people that they were going to really, *really* like the food we were serving because there was only one option on the menu. And I was very good at convincing people, I was. Jerry Budrick's delivery was flamboyant, almost as if he were acting in a theatrical performance, with exaggerated gestures and a full-lipped, beautiful, expressive face like Malcolm McDowell's in *A Clockwork Orange*. Jerry was notorious—he exuded sophistication but could also be very funny, making jokes with customers and the other waiters and the cooks. Brigitte was her sexy self in her miniskirt and clogs, John Harris was erudite and wild about garlic, and Sharon was utterly charming, winning people over. Our waiters did a lot more than most: they cut the bread, tossed the salad, and even stepped in to cook the tarts when needed.

We were vastly overstaffed in the dining room, but it didn't help—none of us had experience handling that sort of volume. We hadn't planned to serve dinner out on the patio, didn't have a waiter assigned to those tables, but it was taking so long to serve people *inside* that we started seating people for dinner *outside*. And that, of course, made it even *more* difficult to serve everyone in a timely fashion. At one point that first night when I was running down the steps to get to the customers on the patio, I tripped and grabbed the railing just in time to stop myself from falling. I could have really hurt myself, and I thought, *Oh my God, that would have been awful.*

I have a distinct memory of looking into the kitchen and feeling so worried about getting the food out on time. Whole roasted ducks were coming out of the oven, and Victoria was smoking a cigarette as she poured off the fat and spooned the sauce over the duck. (Eleanor said that after that night I never stopped smelling of duck fat.) She had made a classic French *sauce espagnole* out of the heads, necks, and feet. I felt a deep panic as I watched: *Are we going to get the duck to the table on time?* I was relieved that the *pâté en croûte* looked as good as it did—with pickles, parsley, and a little mustard arranged on the plate—and was a cold dish, done in advance. I think everyone liked the dinner well enough, but the big hit was Lindsey's plum tart. Which, of course, we ran out of before the night was through.

It was chaos—as Victoria put it, "It was a clown show." We'd wanted the restaurant to feel like eating at home, so we'd resisted getting big industrial tools and appliances and serving equipment—all those things that make life easier that we ultimately had to figure out. We didn't have enough places to set down the dirty dishes or enough space to wash them. We brought everything out on plates one by one instead of bringing the dishes to a bus station—we'd resisted a bus station, too—which meant many more trips in and out of the kitchen. We had a swinging door into the dining room, with a little diamond-shaped window in it, but there's a real learning curve with a swinging door—just imagine how much food dropped on the ground because we didn't know to look through the door to see who was rushing in from the other side!

The food did get to the table somehow, eventually, and people reported having a good time. But it was mayhem; some customers ate on the steps outside. Greil told me later that he arrived at nine and was pleasantly surprised that the food came promptly a few minutes later. But people at the tables around him weren't smiling. "This is the first food we've seen in two hours," they told him.

When I was getting ready to go home that night, deliriously tired, I realized somebody had stolen Martine's artwork off the tree out front. It was so beautiful, it was obvious why they'd taken it; I wonder where it is now. At the end of service, there was no formal celebration. It was more like: *Oh my God. Half the people didn't get food in any sort of a timely way. And what are we going to serve tomorrow?* We didn't want to think about that—so as I always did after a hard day, I opened a bottle of *fumé blanc,* and we toasted getting through the night.

## *La famille Panisse*

I always joked with Bob Scheer that when he lost his bid for Congress, I was so disappointed that I opened Chez Panisse. I was deeply disillusioned about politics, and by opening the restaurant, I really thought that I was dropping out—I was going to do my own thing, no politics, just my little place. But it became political. Because as it turned out, food is the *most* political thing in all our lives. Eating is an everyday experience, and the decisions we make about what we eat have daily consequences. And those daily consequences can change the world.

When people started saying we were doing something revolutionary at Chez Panisse, it thrilled me. When they recognized us as part of the counterculture, the aftermath of the Free Speech Movement, it empowered me; it empowered all of us. We were definitely in that wave, the euphoria of that time that was like "If you want to do something, just *do it!*" The message was "We'll all come and support you!" As panicked as I was in those early days, I felt very supported. It was the way everything was framed—we were in a counterculture movement, united against these big institutions and cultural constructs, but were helping each other. We felt we were doing the right thing, even if we didn't make any money.

I knew very well that I was running a counterculture restaurant, and that Chez Panisse would never have happened without that movement. I couldn't have done it in the real world; the idea of having only one menu was preposterous by mainstream standards, and I never could have borrowed money from the banks. But everybody in the counterculture felt that if you did something *really* well, however unorthodox, if you stayed true to human principles, you could succeed. From the very beginning, it was like that. We had a different set of values. Our place didn't look like other places. We bought used furniture and put mismatched vintage glassware on the table. We hired women as cooks and as waitstaff in a fine-dining establishment, which was practically unheard of at the time. The women and men we hired didn't have long cooking résumés but were smart and talented and believed in the vision. They were intellectuals, writers, would-be filmmakers, and artists; they had no experience but understood our idea and needed jobs. And I was ready to hire them.

All across the country, similar counterculture businesses were opening—we happened to be one of the first restaurants. Other places cropped up in other fertile areas, but Berkeley and the Bay Area happened to be more fertile than

most. We were lucky, because we had the sophisticated cli-
entele of the university, well-traveled people who had been
to Europe and understood what a fixed-price menu was and
were willing to take a chance. And we had had Julia Child
pave the way for French cooking.

We didn't think we should step away from culinary history; why not learn from the past about what really works?
Lamb really *does* work well with beans, it's stood the test
of time. We had all picked up a respect for history. But the
counterculture opened us up to the possibility that we *could*
do things differently, if we saw a better path. Maybe, we
speculated, lamb could work with fresh fava beans in the
springtime instead of traditional dried beans? That was the
great thing about the United States: we didn't have centuries
of culinary tradition to constrain us, so once we learned the
basic techniques, we could improvise. It was liberating to be
freed from the chains of gastronomy. We could use all the elements of French cooking but in our own way. And because
of the counterculture, I could run my kitchen as I wanted,
and do so as a woman. It was pretty rare for a woman to own
and run a restaurant then.

Being part of the counterculture helped keep us alive.
Tom probably brought every single alternative-thinking
person he knew to the restaurant and said, "This is the best
restaurant in the world. Tell all your friends." He brought
every underground filmmaker there and made it a radical
gathering place. He made it his salon; so did David. From

the beginning, there was always a mix of culture and art at
the restaurant. In those early days, we showed the Pagnol
films upstairs after dinner: Tom brought his projector, and
we moved the tables aside, put up a screen, and settled in.

I've always felt like opening the restaurant was fated,
that I didn't have a choice about whether to do it—that it
was somehow predestined. We started out in that world-
changing era of the 1960s, and I wanted something bigger
to happen in my life, something I could be part of. First it
was politics, then it was Montessori, then it was cooking.
I'd always had strong opinions since I was little, and I've always relied on my intuition—a decision has to *feel* right. It's
something I've never worked out intellectually. Is that what
people mean by a calling? My calling may have been to listen
to my intuition. I've followed it my whole life.

A lot of why Chez Panisse succeeded was because it
*didn't* feel like just another restaurant. We were a family—or
at least an eccentric, tight-knit tribe. None of us had ever
been trained as cooks or gone to cooking school. As James
Beard said later, "It's like you're eating dinner in somebody's
home." I wanted it to feel like that.

I've always thought of the restaurant like a child growing
up. During the first years, you know what that's like—you're
panicked: *How am I going to take care of this little baby?* You've
never been a parent before, and you have to be vigilant day
and night. You get no sleep. Then the baby turns three and
starts talking back to you, and you start understanding each

other. When they finally make it to five, they go off to school. Then come beautiful years of sailing along, where everything seems possible. When you make it to ten, you know things are going to be okay. But then people start leaving the restaurant to open their own places, and you panic that you'll have to learn everything all over again—it's like having a teenager. That was when we opened the café upstairs, and the whole operation turned into something more complex. And then you get to twenty, and your child is going out in the world, and it's a bigger world; that's around when I started the Edible Schoolyard Project. At thirty, you feel like the child has its own existence, has an independent life of its own. (And yet your child still calls you on the phone every day for advice and money!) And then your child gets to be forty-five! I always think of Chez Panisse that way.

To be honest, I've never thought of the restaurant as my place. I've always felt, truly, from day one, that it was really Panisse's place, and we were all just stewards of his vision. When I say that, I mean that a larger guiding spirit has always been there, one that's personified by Panisse, a spirit that's bigger than all of us who've worked there. It's the spirit of Pagnol. I heard what those films and books were saying. It was completely relevant to what was happening in the 1960s and '70s, and it's completely relevant to what's happening in our world today. We're leaving the land behind, we're going into the cities, we're losing our traditions of family and friends, we're forgetting about our children, and we're not learning how to feed ourselves in a fast-food world. That was happening in Pagnol's time, and it's why every French schoolchild reads Pagnol's *My Mother's Castle* and *My Father's Glory*. The same values we all hold so dear are articulated and embedded in those works and in all those characters on the docks of Marseille. Like them, we long to live our lives in the most human and beautiful ways possible. It's why we're all part of *la famille Panisse*.

And when my daughter was born, we named her Fanny.

## ACKNOWLEDGMENTS

Without my two collaborators, Cristina Mueller and Bob Carrau, I would never, ever have found a way to write this book. Their persistent curiosity was the driving force behind the entire project. Over the course of two years, they were variously my interviewers, interlocutors, interrogators, transcribers, and fine-tuners, challenging and guiding me to tell my story the best way I could. I'm full of dazzled gratitude: I'll never be able to thank them eloquently or extravagantly enough.

I am also inexpressibly grateful to all the people who put up with my halting efforts to recapture my past, enduring my out-of-the-blue phone calls and endless questions. Among them are my sisters, Ellen, Susan, and Laura, who filled in so many blanks (they remember our childhood better than I do); my old boyfriends Tom Luddy and David Goines, who were so generous with their unclouded and detailed memories of our relationships; and a long list of dear friends and family from past and present alike who contributed indispensable reminiscence, criticism, and support: Eleanor Bertino, Paul Bertolli, Mark Bittman, Jerry Budrick, Patricia Curtan, Dennis Danaher, Sara Flanders, Jean-Pierre Gorin, Samantha Greenwood, Anne Isaak, Sharon Jones, Betsy Klein, Claude and Martine Labro, Greil and Jenny Marcus, Davia Nelson, Sherry Olsen, Charles and Lindsey Shere, Fanny Singer, Stephen Singer, Claire Sullivan, Malgosia Szemberg, Inigo Thomas, Bob Waks, Cathy Waters, Jacqui West, and Victoria Wise.

My enthusiastic agent, David McCormick, and my patient editor, Pam Krauss, get a stand-alone thank-you paragraph for services above and beyond.

Many, many thanks to Ian Dingman for his cover, and to Martha Blegen for her typographical prowess. And, once more, a heartfelt thank-you to Fritz Streiff, my editorial gadfly, for invaluable finishing touches.